Forever Terry

A Legacy in Letters

Edited by Darrell Fox

VIKING

VIKING

an imprint of Penguin Canada, a division of Penguin Random House Canada Limited

Canada · USA · UK · Ireland · Australia · New Zealand · India · South Africa · China

First published 2020

www.penguinrandomhouse.ca

LIBRARY AND ARCHIVES CANADA CATALOGUING IN PUBLICATION
Title: Forever Terry : a legacy in letters / Darrell Fox.
Names: Fox, Darrell, 1963- compiler.
Identifiers: Canadiana (print) 20200181858 | Canadiana (ebook) 20200181912 |
ISBN 9780735240698   (hardcover) | ISBN 9780735240704 (HTML)
Subjects: LCSH: Fox, Terry, 1958-1981. | LCSH: Fox, Terry, 1958-1981—Influence. |
LCSH: Cancer—Patients—Canada. | LCSH: Runners (Sports)—Canada. | LCSH:
Cancer—Patients—Canada—Biography. | LCSH: Runners (Sports)—Canada—Biography.
Classification: LCC RC265.6.F69 F69 2020 | DDC 362.19699/40092—dc23

Cover and book design: Terri Nimmo
Front cover image: Gail Harvey
Front endpaper image: © Terry Fox Foundation /the Fox family
Back cover image: © Terry Fox Foundation /the Fox family
Back endpaper image: © Colin McConnell /*Toronto Star*, Getty Images

Printed and bound in the U.S.A.

10 9 8 7 6 5 4 3 2 1

Penguin
Random House
VIKING CANADA

For Terry, Betty, and Rolly Fox.
For all Terry Foxers, and each and every
person who has been touched by cancer.

Contents

I want to set an example that will never be forgotten.

TERRY FOX, APRIL 26, 1980

One step, stride, hurdle at a time.

Foreword

Michael Bublé

MICHAEL BUBLÉ IS a multi-Grammy and Juno Award winning singer, songwriter, and global entertainer. He has sold over 60 million records, has had several No.1 records including the iconic mega hit "Home," and has performed for over five million fans during the course of his extraordinary career. He is also a hockey fanatic and humanitarian. He currently lives in Burnaby, B.C., with his family.

Granted we're both B.C. boys, but I can't claim to have had a relationship with Terry Fox. I've certainly heard about him, along with every other Canadian and many around the world. And so I had my doubts about being the right person to write this foreword. But after reading these stories about Terry from people who knew him and by a few of the many he has inspired, here I am. I am here because Terry's heroism offers a life lesson we can all benefit from today, tomorrow, and forever.

We all have our heroes. I have my musical ones—Louis Armstrong, Ella Fitzgerald, Dean Martin, Elvis Presley, Bobby Darin. They set a high standard that inspires me to do great work, to challenge myself to heights I never dreamed I could reach. My personal ones are my children, my grandpa . . . In fact, my entire family inspires me every day to be a better man. Everyone needs their heroes, and these stories of Terry Fox—his passion, determination, focus, and legacy—will engage any human being to understand what it is to overcome impossible obstacles.

No one goes through life without challenges, times when you lose hope, wonder where your faith went, question if you can go on, struggle with why this is happening to you. Often these situations come out of nowhere. Each of us, at some point in our lives, will be required to reach deep into ourselves and hope we can find the strength within to take one more step like Terry did. This book is a way to prepare for when that time comes. By hearing about and learning from the example of the short and beautiful life of Terry Fox, you will be ready.

The Marathon was the ride I never wanted to get off. Watching my brother change the world was irreplaceable.

Introduction

Darrell Fox, on behalf of the Fox family

WHILE I NO longer live in 1980, I go back there every day. I'm always reflecting on the Marathon of Hope, reminiscing about being on the road with Terry and reliving the moments we had together. So much of that year feels like it was just yesterday. And yet forty years have passed. When James McCreath, a loyal Terry Fox Foundation supporter and friend, had the brilliant idea to celebrate this milestone anniversary by compiling a collection of letters honouring Terry, we as a family loved the idea and quickly pulled others on board. As the letters began to roll in, the entire book team was moved to tears. I'm often in touch with a handful of the contributors—including Terry's friends Doug Alward and Rick Hansen—but seeing their words on the page was extremely powerful. Reading memories from the people who knew and loved Terry has been overwhelmingly meaningful. But reading how Terry affected the lives of people who were born *after* the Marathon of Hope has been nothing short of incredible. The letters in this book mean the world to my family—and I know they would mean a lot to Terry. Many of his heroes have said he was theirs, something that would thrill him to no end.

Putting this collection together took me back to 1980, and each and every letter allowed me to bask in the details of who Terry was and what he accomplished. As his younger brother,

I admired many things about Terry, his humility perhaps most of all. The person who started the Marathon of Hope on April 12, 1980, was the same person who stopped outside of Thunder Bay on September 1, even with all the fame and affluence that was thrown his way. I saw it first-hand. Terry never changed, and his ability to stay grounded and focused was one of his greatest attributes. I have such admiration for him, so much that whenever I try to express in words what it was like to be part of the Marathon of Hope, I fall short. Maybe that's because I witnessed a miracle.

I was only seventeen when I joined Terry and his best friend Doug on the trip, and my first plane ride was to Saint John, New Brunswick, where I became the third member of the Marathon of Hope. Every day on the road was intense. It would start with Terry curled up in the fetal position in a sleeping bag on his bed, which was the van's pull-out couch. As Doug drove to the marker identifying the exact spot Terry finished running the day before, Terry was mentally preparing for yet another marathon. You could feel the tension in the van; words were rarely spoken. Terry set the tone for the day; Doug and I understood completely and respected this. I felt so much guilt every morning at five when Terry left the comforts of our van, stepped outside, and faced the darkness. I remained protected and warm inside, while Terry faced whatever elements the day had in store. We saw how every step hurt, and I will never know how he coped with the pain. Many people's memories of the Marathon are of how difficult it was for Terry to run it, but it wasn't all pain and suffering. There were moments during the day, and even more at the end of it, when Terry was set free from running and he relaxed. Terry had a wicked sense of humour, exactly like our father's! Picture early Steve Martin–style humour: funny facial expressions and pranks on unsuspecting Ontario Provincial Police officers and the run's entourage members. Terry always relished the opportunity when asked in a public setting to show how his leg worked. He would reach down grab his good leg at the knee, swing it back and forth, and state "Like this!" while trying to contain his laughter! Those moments were everything to us. There are so many photos of Terry smiling that amazing smile of his, taken during the marathon. Is there a better smile out there? Food fights were aplenty and were likely not appreciated by the restaurant owners who donated the meals. But Doug, Bill Vigars, and I knew the value of Terry laughing. Those moments of lightness carried over and added just a touch more energy for Terry to use the next day, on the next marathon.

Being along for the ride was a privilege. Many times, people asked me and Doug if we were bored out of our minds, just following Terry in the van for ten to twelve hours every day. My answer was always, "No, I'm having the time of my life." To be honest, I was worried about what would happen when the Marathon of Hope came to an end, because every day I spent on the road with Terry felt like being on your favourite amusement park ride and never wanting to get off. It was incredible. I witnessed the impact Terry was having on people of all ages, across all demographics and backgrounds. That's what I enjoyed most. Not only was I able to see Terry run every day but I also watched an entire nation embrace him. I couldn't get enough of it.

The outpouring of love was remarkable, and we are as grateful for it now as we were in 1980. When we reached out to the people who so kindly agreed to write a piece for this book, their responses were overwhelmingly enthusiastic. Seeing how much love Canadians still have for Terry has warmed us as a family. Our parents, Betty and Rolland Fox, are no longer with us, but we know they would have taken great joy in this project. Though it's difficult to not have them here for the run's fortieth anniversary, we know life moves on. Just as we've had to live without Terry, we're now moving on without our parents. Thankfully, we have a legion of Terry Foxers, as we call volunteers and supporters of the Terry Fox Foundation, whom we consider family. Many of them are in this book. I'd like to acknowledge our forty-three phenomenal contributors for generously sharing their thoughts and words in this collection; we consider each of you a member of the Fox family, and we thank you for keeping Terry's spirit alive. I also can't thank James McCreath enough. We are beyond grateful for everything you've done to champion this book, James, and we feel so lucky to have you in our fold.

People often recognize our family for what we're doing to honour Terry, to advance his dream of finding a cure for cancer. But we are not the reason his legacy and the Terry Fox Foundation are vibrant. It's because Canadians from east to west and north to south have picked up Terry's baton. You have been running and raising money for him since 1980. You have taught younger generations about what he did and stood for. And you have given our family hope and determination to finish what Terry started, both in times of optimism and happiness and in times when our confidence was failing and we really needed the support. Our family is truly humbled, and we can never thank you enough. We may move through life missing Terry, but we know we are not alone.

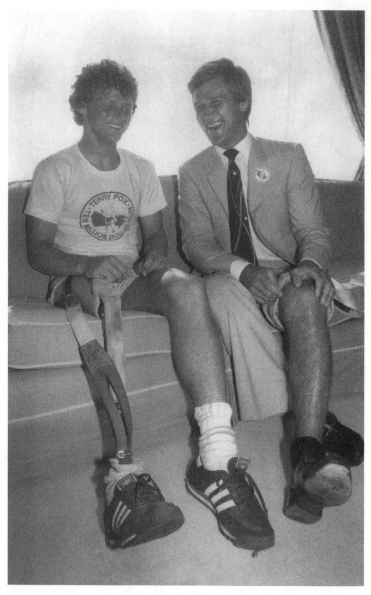

A Canadian worthy of the title of hero, one that I am honoured to have met.

Bobby Orr

BORN IN PARRY SOUND, Ontario, Bobby Orr played professional hockey for the Boston Bruins and Chicago Blackhawks
in the 1960s and '70s, and he helped lead the Bruins to Stanley
Cup victory twice. His speed, scoring, and playmaking abilities
revolutionized the position of defenceman, and he is widely
regarded as one of the greatest hockey players of all time. He
was inducted into the Hockey Hall of Fame in 1979.

Terry Fox touched all Canadians in a way rarely seen in this
country, and it was a wonderful experience for me to get
to meet Terry and his family. That his Marathon of Hope
occurred forty years ago is hard to fathom—it seems like only
yesterday for those of us fortunate enough to have experienced
the event.

I remember we were having lunch in Toronto, and Terry
suddenly had the idea that we should compare our injured
legs. So, I obliged by rolling up my pant leg to just above the
knee and showed him my scars from multiple surgeries. He
returned the favour and I got to see what he was using for a
right leg. It was a very sobering moment. I remember thinking
how courageous this young man must be, given the difficulty
of running with that artificial limb. And for that one moment

in time, my surgeries weren't that important, and those scars
that marked my knee didn't seem so daunting.

We tend to overuse the word "hero" these days, especially
as it relates to sports figures. But the fact that we still honour the memory of this great Canadian four decades later is
a testament to the fact that he is someone truly worthy of the
title "hero."

Whenever I reflect on Terry's accomplishments and consider what he achieved despite his disability, it truly amazes
me. He would run—or walk or hop or limp, whatever he
needed to do—the equivalent of a marathon each and every
day during his time on the highways of Canada. Just consider
that for a moment: a marathon a day for a young man with
one leg who was fighting cancer at the same time. I once read
that it took him about twenty minutes of running each of
those 143 days before he was able to accept the pain that came
along with the activity, and then he would simply bear down
and run yet another marathon. Yes, hero is the right word for
Terry Fox.

Before he ran through my hometown of Parry Sound, my
dad gave me a call and asked, "What can we give Terry when he
comes this way?" I told him to give him anything he thought
was appropriate, so Terry ended up with my Team Canada
jersey from the 1976 Canada Cup. But in truth, I wish I could
have given him a lot more than just a memento.

During the 2010 Winter Olympics in Vancouver, it was my
honour to walk with his mom, Betty, as we carried the Olympic
flag into the stadium during the opening ceremonies. She was

a wonderful lady, and anyone who had the chance to meet her or Terry's dad, Rolly, could see the influence they had had on their son. The family support was evident, and the outcome of that support changed our country for the better.

We take a lot for granted. The everyday act of getting up in the morning, pulling on our socks, and slipping into a pair of shoes is no big deal for most people. We forget how fortunate we are in many respects. Terry's run shone a timely spotlight on how our needs may differ from others' and on those people who find many of the mundane tasks of living a very big deal indeed.

In those forty years since his gallant attempt to cross the country he loved on little more than one leg and a lot of faith, Terry's journey has helped countless Canadians. It should come as no surprise that the significant funding raised through the Terry Fox Runs over the decades has had a major impact on cancer research and treatment. But perhaps even greater than the dollars and cents, Terry Fox has always represented something fundamentally important for Canadians. Terry represents hope. He could not be kept down, would not be intimidated by the task at hand, and demonstrated tremendous resolve in his attempt to run coast to coast for a cause bigger than himself. Cancer denied him the opportunity to dip his foot in the Pacific Ocean and complete his beautiful plan, but in reality, it was "mission accomplished" in so many other ways.

Now, as we celebrate this dynamic Canadian forty years after his Marathon of Hope began, let's take a moment to reflect on what he did and who he was. Let's make sure that the next generation of Canadian children understand the courage he showed through great adversity. His legacy must live on; he was a person whose achievements in the face of tremendous odds stand as an example for everyone. The next generation of Canadians need to have a ready reply when those pessimists among us state that "one person can't really make a difference." The response can be found in two simple words.

Terry Fox.

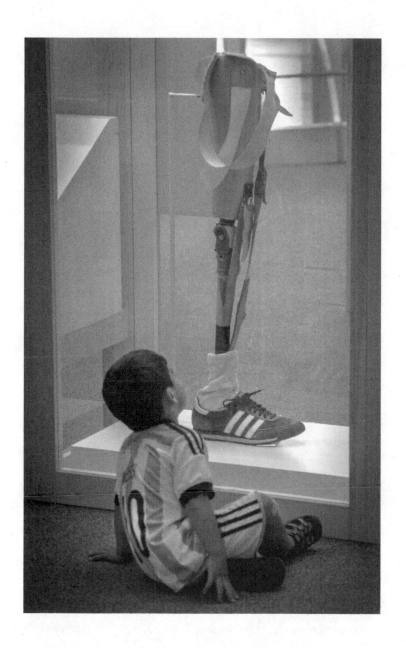

I rarely have been as moved by a single experience in my life, as I was by watching Terry run.

Tom Cochrane

LEGENDARY CANADIAN SINGER-SONGWRITER Tom Cochrane has been inducted into the Canadian Music Hall of Fame and Canada's Walk of Fame. Renowned for both his solo career and the band Red Rider, he is the recipient of eight Juno awards and is an officer in the Order of Canada. Throughout his career, Tom has thrown considerable support behind a wide range of worthy causes.

Sometimes there are seminal moments in life that are cathartic: sometimes big, sometimes small, forks in the road that maybe define who you are and change your course, your direction for life. One of these moments that kick you in the ass happened for me in the late summer, early fall of 1980.

I woke up early one morning leaning against the window in the back seat of a station wagon; a light rain was falling. I was driving with my band Red Rider overnight from a show in Winnipeg to Toronto as we had so many times through that spring and summer after an intense year of touring our first record, *Don't Fight It*. Although the record had been a success in Canada, achieving gold status, and "White Hot" had reached number forty-five on the Billboard chart in the

States, we were—as most bands were early in their careers—in debt, living a vagabond-musician lifestyle of cheap motels, sleeping in the station wagon most nights, eating McDonald's and KFC, taking turns driving through the night to the next show.

Leaning against the window in that station wagon, I was thinking, "What kind of life is this? I've got to do something else. This is no way to live, this isn't for me." All the classic "poor pitiful me" self-doubts that a young man sometimes goes through.

I was thinking, "Now what? We're just a few hours outside of Thunder Bay and the traffic had stopped?" I was pissed. Then slowly, through the early morning greyness and light rain, I saw a police car on the other side of the road moving ever so slowly and just a ways behind was a figure. It took a minute or two to come into focus. It was a boy running with one leg.

As he moved closer, I could see his face. On that face were written a thousand stories, etched on it from every mile that he ran.

Through the drops of water on the glass, I could see the intense determination that was there, the pain, the laboured effort, the courage, and I couldn't tell whether it was sweat, rain, or perhaps a few tears running down his face.

I rarely have been as moved by a single experience in my life.

It was intense. I thought about it for days after. I thought, "How tough is what I'm doing?" It was like a diamond bullet to my soul.

I was blessed to be able to write songs and play music, to make people laugh, smile, dance, and feel a little less alone in this world. I never looked back.

(I think one of the biggest fears in a young person's heart is the idea that they might leave this Earth, this mortal coil, without leaving a mark, without making a difference, without being remembered. Perhaps this had occurred to Terry—after all, he was human—but the selflessness and the profound courage it took for him to dip his foot in the water of the Atlantic and start his monumentally impossible task far supersedes that.)

So Terry ran. He did what came naturally to him to fight for freedom.

Freedom from a disease for himself and for others.

He left a huge mark on this world; he made a difference.

I saw Terry on the morning of the last day that he ran. And though I never got to meet him, I feel, like millions do, that I do know him.

That deep down in that part of us that is good and brave, he resonates with us all as human beings and helps define us as Canadians.

Terry has been a deep inspiration for my course in life. I often wonder what I would be doing if I hadn't seen him running that morning.

We can't help but look at the heroic effort he made, and we will remember him and we will say, "Well done, Terry, well done, and thank you."

I wrote a song some years ago inspired by Terry and had the deep honour of performing it at his posthumous induction into Canada's Walk of Fame with the blessings of Darrell Fox and his family. His brother Darrell had been with him almost the whole way.

rain streaming down early one morning
all down the windowsill there was no warning
traffic stopped what was this
a one-legged boy running like a ghost in the mist

and I saw a look in his eyes like I'd never seen
on the face of any man
a man with a mission before he left the scene
that was the last day that Terry ran

the ones that I've known and the ones that have moved on
the ones that payed the price and the ones that are done
the ones that have stayed the course and gave so much
for freedom
I'll remember the ones and say well done

"The Ones That I've Known," Thomas William Cochrane.

*April 12, 1980, at St. John's Harbour, just before Terry started on his
miraculous marathon.*

Doug Alward

DOUG ALWARD WAS one of Terry Fox's closest friends from childhood and accompanied him on the Marathon of Hope. To this day, Doug is devoted to keeping Terry's dream alive.

"I am just one member of the Marathon of Hope. If I don't make it, the Marathon of Hope better continue." Terry Fox said these prophetic words on July 11, 1980, at the Scarborough Centre near Toronto. Terry's cross-Canada run came to an end in Thunder Bay, Ontario, on September 1, 1980, two-thirds of the way across Canada. His dream continues in the hearts of millions of participants worldwide who have become members of the Marathon of Hope. I am one member of the Marathon of Hope. I had the privilege of being asked by Terry to accompany him on his run across Canada.

From the time we became friends at age ten, we played sports and studied together. We competed hard against each other in soccer, running, basketball, school exams, and every other activity we could think of. I was best at running. Terry became best at basketball. Academically, we were tied. In wrestling, he pinned me to the mat. He had practised with his dad and brothers, which I thought gave him an unfair advantage.

When Terry came up with the idea of running across Canada to raise money for cancer research, he phoned me for advice. I had been a B.C. high school cross-country silver medallist. My first thought was, "I couldn't get you to come run a twenty-minute race on our high school cross-country team when you had two legs. How do you expect to run a forty-two-kilometre marathon every day on one leg?" However, I had already seen Terry do the seemingly impossible over and over again. When we were in grade eight, everyone, including me, thought he was the worst basketball player in all of Canada. Yet he loved the sport. Five years later, after thousands of hours of practice, he stunned us all by making the Simon Fraser University basketball team.

My only training advice to Terry was to start with a tiny bit of running—just one lap of the track—and slowly add more every day. We figured it would take three years to work up to forty kilometres a day, as the body would have to adjust to the pounding and stress. But only one year later, after 5,000 kilometres of training, Terry was running forty kilometres a day. He persevered through shin splints, bone bruises, ankle sprains, and blisters on his stump. Moreover, he was doing all this running while he was a university student and training on the national wheelchair basketball team, with world champion Rick Hansen.

On April 12, 1980, Terry started the cross-Canada run in St. John's, Newfoundland. Our plan was that I would give Terry water and a piece of orange at every mile as he ran to the van. I decided I would keep fit by running a little bit of each mile.

The first time I tried, I ran toward Terry a short distance
then turned back for the van. What a shock. The wind almost
knocked me down! In five minutes, I felt I would freeze to
death. I handed Terry his water and orange, jumped in the van
to get warm, and never got out to run again until we arrived in
Toronto three months later. No one had told us that in April it
was still winter in Newfoundland. That the wind blows from
west to east. That Canada is a series of hills, mountains, and
busy highways with massive freight trucks blasting by, blow-
ing us off the road. That we would often have to travel over
100 kilometres to get to the next town for gas, food, and water.
We were young and naive.

For 143 days, Terry ran nearly forty kilometres a day. Plus,
he did fundraising events on top of the daily run and spoke at
schools and city events. At the time, though I thought Terry
had done a good job, I was puzzled that people were so passionate about Terry's 5,373 kilometres of running. When an
ordinary guy who is your best friend does something incredible, you can't see why it is such a big deal. I had seen Terry do
amazing things his whole life.

Now forty years later, I understand why people thought
Terry's achievement was extraordinary. In fact, I would say
it was miraculous. Terry was capable of running a marathon
three hours faster than the amputee world record at the time.
Terry's primitive artificial limb cost $700. Today, bionic
limbs that allow a near-average running gait cost upwards of
$50,000. Yet no amputee has come close to running as far in
such a short time. Moreover, Terry did so while cancer cells

were growing in his lungs! Terry's run was a miraculous athletic achievement. Now I understand why he was given the Lou Marsh Memorial Trophy, awarded annually to Canada's top athlete, and inducted into Canada's Sports Hall of Fame. The ability to accomplish what Terry did required not only physical stamina but also an unwavering belief in what he was doing.

I watched Terry run at record speed to exhaustion each day. I am convinced Terry was willing to die to help others with cancer. A hero? Terry said, "People in the cancer clinics are the heroes. I am only one member of the Marathon of Hope. Equal with all of you."

Darrell, Terry, and myself, in Quebec City.

It feels like Terry's initial burst of energy when he started his marathon never gave out. He carried the same dedication and passion through his entire run.

Marissa Papaconstantinou

MARISSA PAPACONSTANTINOU IS a Paralympic athlete who specializes in 100-metre and 200-metre sprints. She made her Paralympic Games debut in Rio de Janeiro in 2016 and has represented Canada at three World Para Athletics Championships. The twenty-year-old athlete is currently studying sport media at Ryerson University in Toronto, Ontario.

The biggest part of sprinting is that first step. When I get to the starting line, I try to stay very calm, almost blank-minded, because my body has to focus on reacting to the starter's gunshot. I need to pop out and get that initial burst, otherwise my race is over from the beginning. My body takes over from there. To me, that's the biggest difference between sprinters and long-distance runners: they have to worry about exhaustion, whereas I need to be fast. Not that I don't have my own physical exhaustion to contend with. I spend a lot of time at physio and medical appointments to keep my body healthy, because being an amputee creates all kinds of wear and tear on the body. I'm beyond fortunate, as are so many other amputees, to have amazing technology at our disposal today. My running blade is light and made to replicate the springiness of a biological leg.

That's what astounds me most about Terry's run: his prosthetic leg was made mostly of wood. It was not designed to absorb any of the impact from running. To me, the fact he ran on a basic prosthetic for as long as he did puts him in a whole other category of legend.

When I was growing up, Terry was one of the only people I could relate to. I was born without a right foot and didn't come across many other amputees in Scarborough. Terry was the very first person I saw with a disability who was in the public eye, and seeing him and his prosthetic leg gave me an image of perseverance to hold on to. I've had a lot of challenges in my life and have been through plenty of learning experiences, but Terry taught me at an early age to never give up. I learned about his story at school and from my parents, who got me involved in athletics when I was three years old. They encouraged me to tackle anything I was interested in, so I did soccer, tennis, dance, skiing, and gymnastics, all using my regular prosthetic leg. I got my first running blade when I was twelve and immediately joined a local track club. I started to train with a coach, and when I was thirteen, I broke the Canadian record for the 100-metre sprint. From that moment on, I knew I would strive to achieve a lot more in the sport.

I've had some setbacks that broke my heart, like getting disqualified from the 200-metre race at the 2016 Paralympic Games for stepping on the line, but I think about Terry when things aren't going my way. So many people have faced bigger challenges than I'll ever have to—and Terry Fox is one of them. He was incredibly brave in dealing with his sickness and his

above-the-knee amputation, which is completely different
than my situation. Retaining a knee joint is much easier on
the body than having an artificial one. Often times, above-
knee amputees walk with a swinging motion that can be hard
on the back, hips, and overall energy level, whereas my own
gait can look "normal." Picturing Terry running with his
swinging gait still inspires me today. He reminds me that I am
able to face any obstacle with courage and humility.

Terry was so young when he started the Marathon of Hope.
I often wonder what he thought as he ran all those kilometres,
day after day. I was a naive fifteen-year-old when I started to
race competitively. Ironically, that was when I was the most
relaxed in competition, because I just didn't know any better.
When I started to gain a bit of attention, I felt that people had
expectations of me and struggled with the mental aspect of
competing. I had so many more things running through my
mind. After I was disqualified in Rio and after I tore my ham-
string in London in 2017, I started to wonder, "Can I really
do this?" I spent a lot of time reflecting and realized Terry
must have asked himself that same question. Not only did he
struggle through hard times but he also did so in a national
spotlight. He dug deep, committed to his dream, and made
it happen. I've tried to use Terry's example to quiet my own
self-doubt. As a result, I've been feeling more confident and
relaxed. Ultimately, I'm having more fun because of it.

Terry showed the world that amputees can be powerful,
strong, and resilient. He showed a little girl born without a
right foot that she could be that way, too.

Along the way I hope that I can give inspiration, encouragement, and courage to other people not only to healthy ones but also disabled and those with diseases such as cancer.

Terry's handwriting from a personal letter, dated May 8, 1979, before he had shared his plans to run across the country to raise money for cancer research.

Donna Ball

DONNA BALL WAS a friend and is a long-time supporter of
Terry, his dream, and his legacy. A lifelong volunteer for many
organizations, including the Terry Fox Foundation, she is
enjoying retirement and diving into creative writing.

Terry and I met in St. John's, where I was living and he was
visiting, in the summer of 1978. When he returned to B.C., I
wrote him a letter. We corresponded as pen pals through the
spring of 1979 from the bookends of this great country. Here is
a compilation of excerpts from his letters, followed by a letter I
wrote him on the fortieth anniversary of his Marathon of Hope.

Spring 1979

Dear Donna,
My name is Terry Fox. You wrote me a letter around six
months ago. After telling you a bit more about myself, I
will be able to explain to you why it took so long for me
to write back.
   It's only been two years now since I lost my leg. Sports
had always been the most important part of my life.

Basketball has always been my favourite sport and it was the sport I have also been best at. In 1975–76, I entered Simon Fraser University taking sciences and hoping to make the basketball team. Fortunately I was able to make the junior varsity team. Toward the end of the season, I noticed a pain in my knee that grew worse all the time. The pain got so bad that one morning I woke up and could no longer walk. It turned out that I had cancer and my leg had to be amputated ½ way up my thigh. I was told I had a 50–70% chance to live and that I would have to go on extensive chemotherapy treatments for 1½ years. These were treatments that would prevent, hopefully, the cancer from spreading in the blood. These treatments also made me very sick and also I had temporarily lost my hair.

This event has had the greatest of any impacts upon my life. Although that year and ½ was very tough on me, it was a period of time in which I had gained much courage. With help from so many people, I had always a positive attitude toward the outcome of my treatments and I was able to go on living happily despite the circumstance. I have now been off treatment for a full year. My hair grew in curly when before it was straight.

I really can't explain what impact the hospital atmosphere has had on me. I now have an inner drive to try and help people in terminal situations, not only in diseases such as cancer but all those people who are having problems grasping the meaning of life. It really bothers me to see people living their life with no desires or hopes, and it bothers me to see people in such pain and anguish as those with terminal cancer.

The first twenty years of my life I had been very self-oriented. I had no concerns for anybody but my own well-being. It took cancer and helpful loving people as yourself to realize that being self-centred is not the way to live. The answer is to try and help others.

I've always wanted to be a more loving helpful person. I have realized my athletic efforts can be used to help other people. I know that I have inspired many of my former able-bodied teammates and friends. So I think through athletics I can help other people in troublesome situations by showing them courage and strength to get over the roughest situations.

I have started running with my artificial limb. Every nine days I add on another ½ mile. Right now I am up to running four miles a day. Since my body is very prone to injuries because of my running technique, I also weightlift every day and push my wheelchair up a mountain every second day. My first goal is to run in marathons. My second goal is to try and raise money for disabled sports as well as cancer research. I hope through my efforts I can inspire and help all those people in stressful life situations.

So you can see that the reason I didn't write you before now was that I was too self-centred. I never threw away your letter because I felt there would be a day when I would

want to write back to you. I have nothing but admiration
and respect for people such as yourself. You live your lives
to help others.

Terry

Spring 2020

Dear Terry,
My name is Donna Ball. You wrote me two letters around
forty years ago. After telling you a bit more about the past
few decades, I will be able to explain why it took so long to
write back.

So much has happened since we last talked in St. John's in
April 1980. You know that your goal of raising $24 million for
cancer research was realized. But now almost $800 million
has been raised. That's about one dollar for every North and
South American, not only one dollar for every Canadian.
That money has gone to good use, funding our brightest
researchers across the country to answer the tough questions
about the causes, diagnoses, and treatments of cancer. The
newest research focuses on individualized treatments based
on patients' unique genetic makeups. We have not let your
dream die; lives are saved because of you, and millions are
thankful to you.

Two generations have been born since we last saw each
other. Your story is history for them. How honoured the
rest of us feel to have experienced the Marathon of Hope.
There are statues, schools, stamps, coins, plaques, and

tributes to you everywhere. You are Canada's greatest hero. You united our country and continue to remind us of how great Canada is, the strength of all its peoples. I call you an inclusive visionary. You have inspired, encouraged, and given strength to so many—cancer patients, medical researchers, musicians, athletes (both able-bodied and para-athletes), and people of all ages.

Your family has devoted forty years to your dream. Your mother worked tirelessly and became one of Canada's most admired mothers. People saw your spirit in her. Your dad was so funny. Your siblings are pretty awesome too, as well as your nieces and nephews. I've really enjoyed getting to know your family.

I never threw away your letters because I felt there would come a day when I'd want to share your powerful words. Knowing how much you cared about children, I read them aloud in schools and children's groups. I hope future generations learn from your pure selflessness. I hope they learn that not everyone is going to be a famous Canadian hero, but that we can all make a difference in other people's lives. And I hope they learn that whenever they are experiencing challenging or tough times, they can find a way forward, one step at a time.

Very few days have passed in my life when I haven't thought of you. I remain deeply grateful for our friendship. I have nothing but admiration and respect for you. You lived your life for others.

Donna

The emotions each scene evoked in all of us were astounding—the legacy and memories Terry left us with motivate us to be bigger than we thought we could be, and do more than we ever dreamed we could.

Shawn Ashmore

SHAWN ASHMORE IS a film and television actor from British Columbia. He is best known for his roles as Bobby Drake (Iceman) in the *X-Men* film series; Jake Berenson in the television series *Animorphs*; Agent Mike Weston in the television drama series *The Following*; and, of course, as Terry Fox in the movie *Terry*.

I grew up in St. Albert, Alberta, where I did the Terry Fox Run every year. It was such a big part of growing up. I can remember being proud of Terry, this young man who did something so incredibly difficult and noble. I was too young to really understand it, but I felt the swell of pride that all Canadians feel when they think of Terry Fox. Cut to years later, when I was living and working as an actor in the United States. I received a call saying there was interest in me playing Terry Fox in a film called *Terry*. Of course, I was excited, but my instinct was to say no. I was scared. I mean, how could anyone ever do Terry justice? He's a hero. There are statues of him. Our nation reveres him. Playing him was daunting to even think about. Still, I read the script and loved it. My brother— who's also an actor—said, "If you don't do this, I'm going to!" That was his way of saying, "Are you serious? Why wouldn't you take this role on?" That's when I snapped out of my fear and decided to throw myself into it.

First, I needed to meet with Terry's family to hopefully hear from them, "It's okay to do this." And that blessing is what Darrell Fox, Terry's brother, provided for me. We met for coffee in Toronto to get to know each other. I remember having a good feeling as we talked, and that was the final step for me: I could take on the role.

To help prepare me for shooting the film, Darrell gave me a copy of the personal journal Terry had kept while he ran the Marathon of Hope. Terry hadn't written much about his emotions, but he had tracked details that mattered to him on a daily basis: how many push-ups he did in the morning to warm up, how long he could run before he had to break, if he was feeling good about the progress of the run. Before shooting a scene, I'd read the corresponding entry in Terry's journal. That really helped me to infer his mood and create a picture of him day to day. Seeing those notes in his handwriting pulled me into who he was, beyond what we'd all read and seen before.

Like all Canadians, I already knew that what Terry had done was superhuman. Shooting the film, however, gave me a whole new appreciation. On hot summer days, I ran a fraction of what Terry did and with two legs—and I still found it hard. I spoke to professional athletes who said they needed a week to recover after running a marathon; nobody could understand the physical exertion and dedication that Terry put into his run.

It was unfathomable. Everything came into focus for me when we recreated the speech Terry gave at Nathan Phillips Square in Toronto on July 11, 1980. It was an iconic moment, and the square was filled with hundreds of actors. I looked out over the crowd and saw that people were weeping. I hadn't even said anything yet. Just the memory of Terry made people emotional. It was so powerful. That's when I realized the extent to which Terry had influenced and inspired people. Playing him proved to be the most rewarding role of my career.

Terry is a legend, the greatest Canadian ever. There's no question about it. And I think it's easy to forget he was just a kid when he took on this seemingly impossible task. I always tried to keep that in mind when we were shooting *Terry*: that he was a young man, an athlete to the core, doing something he cared about and loved and believed in. He took one step after another, and that snowballed into a whole nation standing behind him. That's why we all beam with pride when we talk about Terry; he represents the best of humanity, the nobility of doing something bigger than ourselves, the courage of trying to achieve the impossible. And what he accomplished in his lifetime now lives on in his legacy, with hundreds of millions of dollars raised in his honour. Terry's sheer will to achieve his dream, which was an act of pure kindness, created something magical. He gave us hope by showing us that nothing is impossible. That's how I carry Terry with me, and always will.

The vastness of our country is hard to grasp, but the vastness of his heart and dedication are unmatched.

Jann Arden

JANN ARDEN IS an award-winning singer, songwriter, broadcaster, actor, author, and social media star. She stars in her own hit TV sitcom, *Jann*; hosts the weekly *Jann Arden Podcast*; and continues to record and tour. She has written four books, including the Canadian bestseller *Feeding My Mother: Comfort and Laughter in the Kitchen as My Mom Lives with Memory Loss.*

It's funny to me—well, maybe not *funny*, but curious perhaps—how often I think about Terry Fox. Every single time I drive across the country in a tour bus and happen upon Thunder Bay, Terry comes blazing into my mind with a huge smile on his face. I think about how long we've been driving and driving and driving; how big our country is, how vast and open and how far it is between gigs, between cities—and then it occurs to me that Terry Fox *ran here from Newfoundland*. I will never not be in awe of that.

We've stopped at his Thunder Bay monument many times. The beautiful statue showing his young face pointed upwards into the sun, into the future. The band and crew climb out of the buses to stretch their legs and shake off the hours, to grab some fresh air, but mostly to stand and look at Terry and marvel at what he did. Everybody has a story of where they were in 1980 when he started to run. The excitement that started to gather around him almost immediately was palpable—the media didn't take long to document his every move—and kids ran along beside him as he jogged into every small town that was in his path. It was like nothing we had ever seen before in our lives, because it *was* something that we'd never seen before in our lives.

His humility was so distinct. The way he spoke, the way he moved through his days with such a mindful dedication to his cause—which became our collective cause to eradicate cancer—touched the most hardened hearts.

He united the country in a way that we hadn't ever experienced and haven't experienced since, in my humble opinion.

None of us can get our heads around it—even all these years later, his Marathon of Hope seems as heroic and as remarkable and as unbelievable as ever. He ran an average of twenty-six miles a day. Any seasoned athlete can tell you that this is unreasonable and unthinkable, and yet Terry made it seem like it was the most normal undertaking in the world. It wasn't, and we all know that. We all shake our heads in heartfelt disbelief because he made us feel so alive and so grateful to call him *ours*.

Terry Fox was ours and we claimed him from coast to coast to coast and we have never been prouder. I cried for a week after he died. I felt like I knew him, like we went to school together and drank beer down at the river and rode bikes around the block and swam at the local pool until we could hardly keep our eyes open.

Terry let us all feel like he belonged to us. Unselfish. Transparent. Altruistic.

I am so grateful that I was alive to serve witness to this young man's life.

The greatest honour of my career—accompanying Terry on his Marathon.

Bill Vigars

AS DIRECTOR OF public relations and fundraising for the
Canadian Cancer Society's Ontario Division, Bill Vigars played
an instrumental role in Terry's run. Not only did he travel with
Terry to organize key media events across the province but also
they became close friends along the way. Bill counts the Marathon of Hope as the most meaningful experience of his career.

I was barely three months into my job at the Canadian Cancer
Society when my boss came into my office with a question that
would change my life. He said, "There's a kid running across
Canada. Do you want to go see what you can do for him?"
I called Terry, and two weeks later, I went out to meet him on
the road. I flew to Quebec City and then drove to Edmundston,
New Brunswick. I didn't arrive until about three in the
morning, so I parked outside of the guys' motel room and
climbed into the back seat of my car to catch a couple hours
of sleep. I woke up to find Terry, his brother Darrell, and his
friend Doug coming out of the motel room. Doug looked at
me incredulously and asked, "You're the guy from the Cancer
Society?" They were used to dealing with suits in their sixties
and here I was, a thirty-three-year-old with bedhead and
rumpled clothes interrupting their morning ritual.

The four of us headed into the motel room so Terry could
drop off some mail and cassettes that I had brought him. A
quick chat later, we all jumped in the van and headed out into
the darkness. Doug drove up and down the road, as we looked
for the white plastic bag they'd partially buried on the side of
the highway the night before. Every morning, they had to pull
up to the exact spot Terry had finished the previous day, so he
could step out of the van and onto the bag. He was insistent
about this: he didn't want anyone to be able to claim that he
didn't run every single step. We left Terry to begin his run.
As was the routine, Doug parked on the side of the road exactly
one mile ahead. We sat in silence and I soon saw Terry in the
rear-view mirror, running toward us. I witnessed the effort
in every step, with that gait of his that I continued to watch for
the next three months. It sucked the breath right out of me.
When he needed a break, nobody talked. Terry would catch
his breath, eat a little something, and head back out. By about
the third mile, after he exited the van, I asked Doug, "How do
you watch him do this?" He replied, "I don't." Initially, I didn't
understand what he meant. I later realized that it was too hard
for Doug to watch his friend put that effort in mile after mile.

As he ran through eastern Canada, more and more people
came out to see Terry run. He'd get to a rural intersection and a
few families would be waiting for him, crying and handing us
donations as we passed through. We would count the money
every night. At first, we wondered why so many of the bills
were crumpled into tight balls. We realized people were standing there with money in their hands, looking down the highway

for Terry. And as they watched him run, they were anxiously balling their hands into fists as they waited, and so crumpling up the bills they were holding.

As Terry was making his way through Quebec, I was busy driving between Toronto and Ottawa to visit every small town in between to let them know he was coming. When he crossed into Ontario, those towns gave him such warm receptions. If a town had 300 people, 600 would show up. The awareness was growing, but I told Terry, "To make it big in Canada, we have to make a splash in Toronto because that's where all the big media is." My theory was we had to make a splash in Ottawa first in order to make an impression in Toronto. We timed it so that Terry was in Ottawa for Canada Day. We didn't have a plan but I was ballsy and thought we'd show up at Parliament Hill and try to get him onstage. We were getting ready to head there when someone from the Ottawa Rough Riders asked if Terry wanted to make the opening kick to start their game. I gave him the choice: take a risk at Parliament Hill or go to the game. He said, "I'd rather go to a football game."

We went and waited underneath the stadium. The lights were off and Terry was practising kicking the ball, afraid he'd fall on his face. Then somebody yelled, "It's time!" and we started up the stairs. As we came out of the tunnel and onto the field, I remember thinking, "I hope they know who he is." As Terry walked to the sidelines, the announcer boomed, "Ladies and gentlemen, please welcome . . ." He didn't even get Terry's name out and the whole place erupted in a standing ovation that went on and on. The next day, as we were starting out at five in the morning, I looked at the newspaper box on the side of the road, and there was Terry on the front page. I put in my fifty cents and took all of the newspapers out. Terry was upset I did that and made me call the newspaper the next day to admit what I'd done. I told the guy everything—he just laughed and said, "Keep them."

From then on, all the media followed Terry's run. Once in a while a reporter would show suspicion, like, "Is this guy too good to be true?" After spending a little time with Terry, they knew he was the real deal. Terry spoke from the heart. There were no two sides to him. As difficult as the Marathon of Hope was, Terry used to tell people, "If I wasn't running across Canada, I'd be running around a track in Port Coquitlam. So, I might as well run across Canada." Happy is not the right word to describe how he felt during the Marathon of Hope, but he was doing it because it was an athletic feat. After he got sick and went home, there was an incredible outpouring of love and respect from across the country. People were naming schools and streets after him. He was very honoured and humbled, of course, but the only time he ever got really excited was the day he was awarded the Lou Marsh Memorial Trophy, awarded annually to Canada's top athlete.

When it came time, saying goodbye to Terry broke my heart. I promised to keep his story alive, and I've tried to do that by telling his story to schoolkids. When I talk about Terry, I don't talk about Terry the hero. I tell them about Terry the kid, who was funny and competitive and a regular guy. He liked to say, "I'm no better than you. I'm no worse than you." Terry may have been a regular guy, but he was a human being like no other. And he was my friend. I will never be able to comprehend how blessed I am in having known and loved him.

It is a great privilege to be an NHL all-star; it takes so much more to be an all-star for humanity, as Terry was.

Darryl Sittler

DARRYL SITTLER IS regarded as one of the greatest players to ever wear the Toronto Maple Leaf uniform. Since his retirement in 1985, he has remained at the top of the Leafs all-time-points and goal-scoring lists; he has been inducted into the Hockey Hall of Fame; and in 1995–96, Darryl was voted by fans as the centreman on a fantasy all-time Leafs team. In 2003, the Leafs retired Darryl's number, 27.

I distinctly remember the day I got a phone call out of the blue asking me if I'd like to meet Terry Fox. It was the summer of 1980, and I'd been following Terry's run since seeing him on the front page of a Toronto newspaper. I remember reading about how he'd dipped his prosthetic leg into the Atlantic Ocean before beginning his run across Canada. His story and that photo of him really grabbed at my emotions. At that time, I was playing for the Toronto Maple Leafs. I knew from my own training what it took to run five or ten miles on two legs, let alone twenty-six miles every day on one leg, through rain, snow, and all kinds of weather. His story really touched my heart, so I began to follow his journey. The day Terry arrived at the Quebec-Ontario border, people from the Ontario Cancer Society greeted him and asked if there was something special they could do to show their appreciation. He said he'd always wanted to meet Bobby Orr or Darryl Sittler. So, when I received the call asking if I'd like to meet Terry and run with him in Toronto, I said, "Oh boy, would I ever love to meet Terry Fox!"

When the day came, I thought, "What's something that I could do to show my appreciation for Terry?" I grabbed my jersey from the NHL all-star game I'd played in earlier that year. Then I drove to downtown Toronto to surprise Terry at his hotel. He'd already finished thirteen miles that morning and was up in his room. He had no idea I was coming. I had my shorts and a Terry Fox T-shirt on, and I walked in and said, "Hey, would you like to go for a run?" I can't recall what he said, but I'll never forget the look on his face. He was tying his shoe and looked up at me with his warm smile and his curly hair, and our eyes connected. I don't know what was going through his head, but for me, the moment was special. As much as he wanted to meet me, I wanted to meet him, and it was perfect.

After that, we prepared a bit for the run and made our way outside. July 11, 1980, was a beautiful, sunny day, and as we started down Avenue Road, I was blown away by the number of people in the street. People were cheering and clapping. Some were in tears. I ran a bit behind Terry and did my best to take in the emotions of the crowd. Even though the streets had been filled with people, I was still surprised to see Nathan Phillips Square packed when we arrived; I hadn't realized the magnitude of Terry's presence. We joined some politicians onstage and that's when I presented Terry with my all-star jersey. To be standing there with him, among thousands of people who were rooting for him, was one of the most extraordinary experiences of my life. Terry's run continued, and we stayed in touch now and then. Like everyone else, I was shocked and devastated to hear his cancer had returned and the run was over.

When the Leafs played in Vancouver some months later, I called and asked Terry if he'd like to come to the dressing room and meet the guys. I was thrilled when he came to our practice, but you could really see the effects the disease and the treatments were having on him; he'd become pale and thin. But what I remember most—and what I always share when I talk about Terry Fox—is how humble he was. It was unbelievable. Terry's mission had nothing to do with ego and everything to do with making a difference in other people's lives. He was shy and modest; to me, humility is one of the greatest qualities any person can have. And what a person he was. What Terry accomplished in his short life has been my inspiration ever since. In my home, I have a copy of Ken Danby's famous painting depicting Terry and me at Nathan Phillips Square. Every day I pass it and think, "Okay, how do I want to live this day, and what can I do to possibly make a difference?"

When Terry lost his leg to cancer, he had a choice: he could feel sorry for himself or he could fight and maybe become an inspiration to others. When he started the Marathon of Hope—his dream of running across Canada twenty-six miles a day, one day at a time—I'm sure he had no idea he was creating a legacy that would continue to inspire us forty years later. But he knew if he sat on the sidelines, nothing would happen. So that has been his message to me, and what I like to share with others: if you get involved and choose to move forward, even in the smallest way, you can make a difference. We can all volunteer, help a neighbour, or pay it forward in some way. That's what Terry Fox taught me, and I will forever be grateful.

Terry Fox, November, 1968.

Fred Fox, Dick Traum, and myself bringing the spirit of Terry and Canada to NYC.

Ken Ottenbreit

KEN OTTENBREIT IS the managing principal of the New York office of Stikeman Elliott, a Canadian law firm. A proud expat, he is a board member and past president of the Canadian Association of New York. Ken is also the founder and organizer of the annual Terry Fox Run in New York City.

I was born in Regina, Saskatchewan, in the same year as Terry Fox. I moved to Toronto to attend law school in September 1980, shortly after Terry had run through the city on his Marathon of Hope. I was very impressed that someone my age was on this incredible journey and inspiring a nation. Terry's run made me want to do more.

After I moved to New York in 1988, I wanted to stay connected to my Canadian roots so I became active in the Canadian Association of New York (CANY). When I became president, my goals were to find a new Canadian-related charitable activity for CANY and for our community to make more of a mark in NYC. I discovered that there had been a Terry Fox Run in London, England, and immediately I knew that we had to bring a run to New York City. This was a chance to do more.

I wanted to have the run in Central Park because it is such a fantastic park and iconic running venue, but soon realized that it would be difficult to get a permit. While I was disappointed, I was determined to get the run started so we held our first run in 1994 in Riverside Park on Manhattan's Upper West Side. For Canadians living outside of the country, participating in an international Terry Fox Run is a wonderful way to show national pride, make a positive contribution, and grow Terry's legacy as we remember this extraordinary Canadian hero. Two of the runs in those early years were during brutal storms but as hearty Canadians honouring a national icon, we did not let rain, wind, and cold deter us. Since 1998, we have held the run in Central Park, which has been huge for garnering attention outside of the expat community.

During the process of moving the run to Central Park, I met with the famous run organizer Fred Lebow, who was the chairman of the New York Road Runners club and founder of the New York City Marathon. He knew some of Terry's story and wanted to learn more about "the one who started this all"—meaning that Terry pioneered the idea of raising money for a cause by running, walking, biking, and so on. Fred saw Terry's run as a groundbreaking idea and considered him to be a visionary trailblazer.

Back when I was planning the first run, I had learned that Terry had been inspired by Dick Traum, a one-legged runner who was the first amputee to finish the New York City Marathon. Dick had joined in the first two Terry Fox Runs in Canada where he saw other athletes with disabilities participating. That inspired Dick to start Achilles International, a worldwide track club for disabled athletes that now has chapters around the world. Every year, hundreds of Achilles athletes participate in the New York City Marathon—another offshoot of Terry's legacy. Dick participated in New York's first Terry Fox Run in '94, and he and a team of Achilles athletes have been there every year since. While Dick never met Terry Fox, it was a great privilege for me to introduce Dick to Betty, Darrell, Judith, and Fred Fox during their visits to Manhattan. One of the great joys of organizing the run is the relationship I have with the Fox family, who carry on and build Terry's amazing legacy.

In 2001, the Terry Fox Run was one of the first runs to take place in Central Park after 9/11. We decided to hold the run because, as Canadians and New Yorkers, we thought it was important to return to our normal activities without fear. We had a glorious day with our best turnout ever up to that point.

People who know the Terry Fox story are very eager to participate in the run, and others who learn about Terry because of our run are inspired and become loyal supporters. In recent years, we have had more than 100 teams participate: teams supporting families and friends with cancer, Canadian university alumni teams, school teams, corporate teams, and others. The run is a great way for Canadian universities to stay connected with their international alumni networks, and every year we have people who travel from Canada to participate in our run. Many of the teams have been active for several years and are very important to our fundraising success. One example is Kate's Team, the extended family of Kate O'Shaughnessy, who died from cancer. She and her family had participated in the Terry Fox Run in Central Park in 1999, and her family runs every year to celebrate her life and to do something positive to remember her. The Terry Fox Run gives them a meaningful outlet for their wonderful energy and commitment to the cause.

The run has become the largest annual event for the Canadian community in NYC. Bringing Canadians together outside of Canada to continue and grow Terry's legacy is a powerful and galvanizing event that gives Canadians an ideal way to show who we are. Canadian expats are always very moved and enthusiastic when they learn about a Terry Fox Run here because they grew up with the story and know what it means. It is something that all Canadians can rally around and proudly share with others. What Terry stands for is what we as Canadians aspire to be. In an often crazy and troubling world, gathering together to participate in the Terry Fox Run is very meaningful individually and collectively. We are doing something important for ourselves and for Canada, and we're grateful to Terry Fox for inspiring us all to do more.

In this day and age, it is often difficult for a diverse group to wholeheartedly support and rally behind any one person or cause, but with Terry Fox, it's easy—he represents a simple but remarkable story of perseverance, courage, and determination that has touched so many lives and stands the test of time.

Terry Fox is a shining example of the difference one person can make. As Canadians, we are very proud of Terry Fox, and it has been an honour and privilege for me and CANY to be a part of the story and to grow Terry's incredible legacy in the Big Apple and beyond.

The only person I've been honoured to lose a game of basketball to—words cannot do justice to what this man has done for the world.

Wayne Gretzky

WAYNE GRETZKY, NICKNAMED "The Great One," is considered
by many to be the greatest hockey player ever. When he retired
from the National Hockey League in 1999, he had played twenty
seasons for four teams—the Edmonton Oilers, Los Angeles
Kings, St. Louis Blues, and New York Rangers—and held sixty-
one of the league's records. Wayne lives in California with his
wife and is still the leading scorer in NHL history.

The first time I met Terry, I didn't realize I was meeting a
young man who was about to become the most influential
Canadian in history. It was the winter of 1979 and I was playing for the Edmonton Oilers. One day, our assistant public
relations director, Elaine Ell, came to the locker room to
ask if Mark Messier, Kevin Lowe, Lee Fogolin, and I would
play in a charity game of wheelchair basketball against Team
Canada. Of course we said yes. Thankfully, Elaine, who used
a wheelchair and was an accomplished Paralympic athlete,
offered to play on our team. Terry Fox and Rick Hansen were
both on Team Canada, and every single player on that team
was amazing. I believe they won the game 44–4, and Elaine
scored both of our baskets.

When Terry started the Marathon of Hope, my father called
to tell me that a man was running from the East Coast to
British Columbia. I didn't realize he was one of the guys who'd
beaten us in wheelchair basketball. I wanted to be there the
day Terry arrived at Nathan Phillips Square and was disappointed I couldn't make it. I knew it would be a great event
not only for the city of Toronto but also for Terry and everyone
involved in the run. When his cancer came back, I was devastated for him and his family, and I wanted to reach out somehow. I had my chance when the Oilers played in Vancouver
near the end of the 1980–81 season. Kevin Lowe and I called
Terry's parents to see if we could visit him at home. As soon
as they said yes, we jumped in a taxi.

Terry felt sick and was resting in bed, but he was upbeat.
He was a huge sports fan and wanted to talk hockey, and he was
actually the one who told us we'd played wheelchair basketball
against each other. We talked a little about his run, too: how
he'd gone through trials and tribulations at the beginning but
how it had turned into something unique and special by the
end. He was disappointed he couldn't finish, but he was doing
everything he could to beat his cancer and get back out there.
I remember him saying he was trying a new drug, as a kind of
guinea pig, because he was willing to do anything to get better
and to help others in his situation. We spent a couple of hours
with Terry that I'll never forget. I found him to be extremely
humble. And even though he felt really tired, he wasn't down.
He wasn't mad. He was full of life, and I enjoyed my entire
conversation with him.

There are certain people who are put on Earth for a reason, and Terry was one of those people. He pushed us to think outside the box, to open our eyes, to get involved, even if we haven't been touched by cancer ourselves. He raised incredible awareness and put cancer research in the forefront of our minds—and he still does today. Thanks to Terry's efforts and the hundreds of millions of dollars that have been raised in his honour, we have new medications and better treatments. Having lost both my mom and sister-in-law to cancer, I am so grateful for him and everything he accomplished. There are no words that can do him justice, no award or monument in Canada that is big enough or good enough to bear his name. Some day, they'll find a cure for cancer. And we'll be able to thank Terry Fox for leading the way.

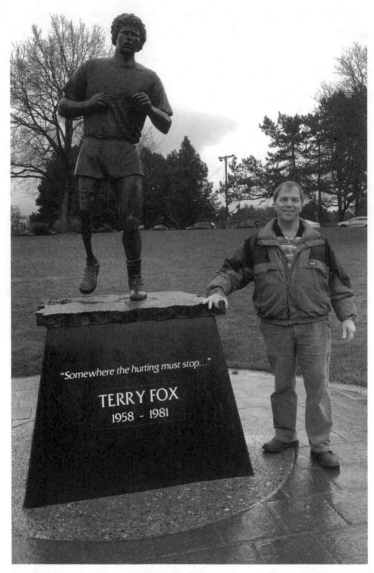

Statue of the man who compelled me to push myself, to take on big challenges, to create awareness and a better future.

Jim Terrion Jr.

JIM TERRION JR. lives in Prince George, B.C., where he works in the housekeeping department at the University Hospital of Northern British Columbia. He was a torchbearer at the 2015 Canada Winter Games in Prince George and has received other honours, including a Terry Fox Run Certificate of Appreciation in 1992 and a BC Achievement Community Award in 2006.

When I saw Terry Fox on TV—he dipped his artificial leg into the Atlantic and then started his run—I thought to myself, "Terry is disabled and so am I." In 1960 I was born deaf, which is a different disability from Terry's but one I've had to deal with my whole life. To know that someone with one leg could tackle a mission so big inspired me. Such ambition wasn't something I had seen before. I felt compelled to be better and to help Terry accomplish his dream of one day finding a cure for cancer.

When Terry began his run, I was in my last year at the Jericho Hill School for the Deaf in Vancouver. I read all the newspaper stories about his progress and kept a journal of what I believed was a historic event in the making. I silently cheered him every step of the way. When my hometown, Prince Rupert, hosted its inaugural Terry Fox Run in

September of the following year, I proudly walked the five kilometres. At the time, I didn't realize the kilometres I logged were just the beginning of my own journey, in many ways.

For ten years, I took part in Prince Rupert's Terry Fox Run. I didn't raise any money but I had plans to someday. There was just something I had to do first. Terry had such a profound impact on me that I decided to start my own cross-country trek, called the Silent Walk, in 1990. My goal was to walk across Canada and back to raise awareness for people with hearing disabilities. I walked 9,917 kilometres over eight months, covering 100 kilometres in one day alone, and raised $150,000 for organizations that help the deaf and the hard of hearing, as well as the Winter Deaflympics. After accomplishing a mission that was close to my heart, I was ready to focus my attention on Terry, the person who'd started it all.

One of the things I learned during the Silent Walk was how to approach people for donations. I put my new skills to use when I began to canvass and fundraise for the Terry Fox Foundation in 1991. My fundraising efforts were slow because it's not always easy for me to communicate with others. I do it by writing notes to my contributors or showing them the clipboard I carry with all my pledge sheets. That first year, I managed to raise $7,586.25 from the generous people in Prince Rupert. I've been fundraising ever since, raising money in both my hometown and Prince George, where I've lived since 2006. I begin fundraising every June in Prince George and take holidays in August and September so I can return to Prince Rupert. I fundraise and take part in the run there, and sometimes I make it back to Prince George in time to participate in its run, too. I enjoy getting everyone involved in fundraising and am very thankful to both communities for the support I receive to fulfill Terry's dream. We have accomplished so much together. To date, I've raised $788,000. My goal is to reach $1 million by 2024.

I've collected Terry Fox newspaper clippings since 1991 and have them in files labelled by year. I have the utmost respect for Terry and everything he went through on his run, and I have pledged my support to keep his dream alive. I, too, want a world free of cancer and the suffering it causes. Like so many people, I have lost family members to cancer, and I will do everything I can to help find a cure. My goal is in sight and I am a very determined person. But even after I meet my goal, I plan to keep walking and fundraising in support of Terry's mission to end cancer for good. My shoes may have covered a lot of ground, but they still have many kilometres left in them.

The embodiment of so many values we hold dear, Saint Terry Fox.

Margaret Atwood

MARGARET ATWOOD, WHOSE work has been published in more than forty-five countries, is the author of more than fifty books of fiction, poetry, critical essays, and graphic novels. In addition to *The Handmaid's Tale*, now an award-winning TV series, and the international bestseller *The Testaments*, her novels include *Cat's Eye*, shortlisted for the 1989 Booker Prize; *Alias Grace*, which won the Giller Prize in Canada and the Premio Mondello in Italy; *The Blind Assassin*, winner of the 2000 Booker Prize; the MaddAddam Trilogy; *The Heart Goes Last*; and *Hag-Seed*. She is the recipient of numerous awards, including the Peace Prize of the German Book Trade, the Franz Kafka International Literary Prize, the PEN Center USA Lifetime Achievement Award, and the Los Angeles Times Innovator's Award.

In Margaret Atwood's brilliant visionary imagining of the future,
The Year of the Flood, *natural disaster has altered the Earth as we know it. The novel not only vividly reflects to us what is familiar in a drastically changed world but poignantly reminds us of our enduring humanity, and in it Atwood features the heroes and saints who have exemplified what we value most, among them Terry Fox.*

SAINT TERRY AND ALL WAYFARERS

YEAR TWENTY-FIVE.

OF THE WANDERING STATE.

SPOKEN BY ADAM ONE.

Dear Friends, dear Fellow Creatures, Fellow Sojourners on this dangerous road that is now our pathway through life:

How long it has been since our last Saint Terry's Day on our beloved Edencliff Rooftop Garden! We did not realize then how much better those times were, compared with the dark days we are living through now. Then, we enjoyed the prospect from our peaceful Garden, and though that prospect was one of slums and crime, yet we viewed it from a space of restoration and renewal, flourishing with innocent Plants and industrious Bees. We raised our voices in song, sure that we would prevail, for our aims were worthy and our methods without malice. So we believed, in our innocence. Many woeful things have happened since, but the Spirit that moved us then is present still.

Saint Terry's Day is dedicated to all Wayfarers—prime among them Saint Terry Fox, who ran so far with one mortal and one metallic leg; who set a shining example of courage in the face of overwhelming odds; who showed what the human body can do in the way of locomotion without fossil fuels; who raced against Mortality, and in the end outran his own Death, and lives on in Memory.

On this day we remember, too, Saint Sojourner Truth, guide of escaping slaves two centuries ago, who walked so many miles with only the stars to guide her; and Saints Shackleton and Crozier, of Antarctic and Arctic fame; and Saint Laurence "Titus" Oates of the Scott Expedition, who hiked where no man had ever hiked before, and who sacrificed himself during a blizzard for the welfare of his companions. Let his immortal last words be an inspiration to us on our journey: "I am just going outside and may be some time."

The Saints of this day are all Wayfarers. They knew so well that it is better to journey than to arrive, as long as we journey in firm faith and for selfless ends. Let us hold that thought in our hearts, my Friends and fellow Voyagers.

. . .

Let us sing.

THE LONGEST MILE

The last mile is the longest mile—
'Tis then we weaken;
We lose the strength to run the race,
We doubt Hope's beacon.

Shall we turn back from this dark Road,
Footsore and weary,
When deep Despair has drained our Faith,
And all seems dreary?

Shall we give up the narrow path,
The plodding byway—
Chose swift transport and false delight:
Destruction's highway?

Shall Enemies erase our Life,
Our Message bury?
And shall they quench in war and strife
The Torch we carry?

Take heart, oh dusty Travellers:
Though you may falter,
Though you be felled along the way,
You'll reach the Altar.

Race on, race on, though eyes grow dim,
And faint the Chorus;
God gives us Nature's green applause—
Such will restore us.

For in the effort is the Goal,
'Tis thus we're treasured:
He knows us by our Pilgrim Soul—
'Tis thus we're measured.

From *The God's Gardeners Oral Hymnbook*

Excerpted from The Year of the Flood *by Margaret Atwood.*

I wasn't able to experience what it was like to be in Terry's presence while he was on this Earth, but we all feel his spirit when we participate in the yearly Terry Fox runs. Here, my family and I are taking part in a run in Prince George.

Nadine Caron

BORN AND RAISED in Kamloops, B.C., Dr. Nadine Caron is a surgeon in Prince George at the University Hospital of Northern British Columbia, an associate professor at the University of British Columbia's Faculty of Medicine, and a founding member of the Terry Fox Research Institute's research advisory commit- tee. As the first female surgeon of First Nations descent, she is passionate about improving Indigenous well-being and serves as founding co-director of UBC's Centre for Excellence in Indigenous Health. Like Terry Fox, Nadine studied kinesiology and played basketball at Simon Fraser University.

I was nine years old when I watched the beginning of the Marathon of Hope on CBC. As the run progressed, I remember sitting on the grass in my backyard with my neighbourhood friends as we planned to be there when Terry passed through Kamloops. I remember talking about Terry at our kitchen table with my brothers and parents, and my request was simple but earnest: when Terry passed through our town, could I be there? I wanted to see him. Cheer him on. I wanted to feel what it was like to be in his presence, if only for a moment. Someone we had never met, who was thousands of kilometres away, brought his message into our house. He was my first hero.

As I grew up, our stories crossed paths many times. We both studied kinesiology at Simon Fraser University and played basketball for "the SFU Clan" atop Burnaby Mountain, although I was there a decade later. When I moved to Prince George, I heard stories about Terry from friends and colleagues; the city takes such pride in its connection to Terry and all he stood for. It's where Terry tested his endurance by running in the Prince George to Boston marathon in '79. Just seven months after testing himself in Prince George, Terry started the Marathon of Hope. Prince George is where I started my career as a cancer surgeon and researcher, and my work led me to join the B.C. research advisory committee of the Terry Fox Research Institute (TFRI), led by Dr. Victor Ling and Dr. Marco Marra. I was honoured to align myself so closely with Terry's mission to eradicate cancer.

The TFRI has been a leader in Canada in facilitating translational research. This means turning scientific discoveries into practical applications. Ultimately, the goal is to develop and implement new ways to prevent, diagnose, and treat cancer. As researchers, our role is not just to identify the issue we have chosen to highlight in a project, grant, or career but to make it understandable to those who can be impacted by it and to make it accessible for those who should benefit from it. Many of our Indigenous populations and people in Canada's northern, rural, and remote areas cannot access our health care system or the research they would benefit from. One of the biggest challenges we face is bringing innovative research studies to marginalized populations, including them as partners, and ensuring equitable access to the subsequent benefits.

One of the main reasons I chose to start my career in Prince George is my passion to provide health care for our northern, rural, and Indigenous populations, and northern B.C. has made that a daily honour. Terry was not fazed by Canada's vast geography and its lonely stretches of highway. When he planned his Marathon of Hope, he went to rural, northern, and remote parts of Canada, along with big cities and small towns. He wanted every Canadian, rich or poor, to donate one dollar. He wanted everyone to benefit equally, too. And everyone should. Terry serves as an example of what we—as researchers, health care providers, and advocates for change—will forever aim to achieve.

Terry's Marathon of Hope was perhaps a research project itself. His objectives were two-fold: to increase awareness of cancer and to raise money for cancer research. His "translational research" was of a different kind from our scientific work. It was not a discovery in genomics, pharmaceuticals, or diagnostic technology. It was something that I believe is so much harder. To all Canadians, he passed on his passion for an endeavour that needed to grow with time, his commitment to a goal, his hope that cancer could be beaten, his belief that cancer research was the vehicle to a better future, and his emotional intelligence that it was okay to love a stranger. Terry showed us that it was human to want to be part of something bigger than yourself.

I was ten years old when Terry passed away. He was the first person who died from cancer that I ever cried for, a disease I found so hard to understand when I was young. I did not know back then that my professional challenge would be to understand small parts of cancer—or that Terry would not be the last person with cancer I would shed tears for. But he moved cancer, a word that so many were afraid to talk about, into our kitchen-table conversations and into our hearts. Surely as researchers and health care providers, we can reach out to our communities—including our marginalized populations—to improve their access to (and quality of) our health care system in Canada. We must develop research methods that include their barriers to cancer care as "questions to be addressed," not as "exclusion criteria."

Access to our health care system and its full spectrum of services is a challenge. In Prince George, we have fought those battles valiantly, we continue to do so, and we are witnessing improvements. But there is an access issue even less talked about: the access to research as a fundamental tool to improving health status, including that in the cancer realm. Terry's goal was to raise money for cancer research, to make a difference, to create solutions. He never said research only for those with his type of cancer or only for those in B.C. He never said research only for people like him, who were his age, his gender, and had the same background. Terry knew this was a fight that needed the whole nation to listen and rise up, because everyone is at risk for this disease—and everyone could potentially benefit from research evaluating its prevention, diagnosis, and treatment. I think that research itself is a determinant of health. Those who are part of it benefit more from it. Those communities who are part of it benefit more from it. Those who are isolated, don't have access, or are left on the sidelines benefit least.

Terry wanted every Canadian to benefit. For this reason, the TFRI is a pan-Canadian research institute. I suspect he would be proud of what we as a country have accomplished so far—but I do not think he would be satisfied until that elusive finish line of conquering cancer has been reached. We continue the course, as Terry did, one step at a time.

Fundraising and promoting the Terry Fox Run in my community, Burnaby, B.C.

Anna Solnickova

ANNA SOLNICKOVA IMMIGRATED to Canada in October 1998 from the Czech Republic. She feels a special connection to Terry as she's a two-time survivor of osteosarcoma, the same cancer that Terry had. Anna is a CPA-designated accountant and lives in Vancouver, B.C., with her husband.

When I moved to Burnaby, B.C., with my family at age thirteen, I spoke about five words of English and had no idea who Terry Fox was. Going through ESL classes and participating in my school's Terry Fox Run introduced me to his Marathon of Hope, but the magnitude of his selfless actions didn't really hit me until a few years later.

After months of excruciating knee pain and countless doctor visits, in 2002 I was diagnosed with osteosarcoma in my right distal femur—bone cancer in my right knee. I was seventeen years old and had just started grade twelve. After the initial shock, my boyfriend (now husband) pointed out that I had the exact same cancer in the exact same location that Terry Fox had when he was eighteen. Naturally, my fear was that, like Terry, I would need an amputation.

Two weeks after the diagnosis, I started chemotherapy; all my hair fell out. I mean, *all* of it, not just on my head but on every inch of my body. You don't realize the importance of eyebrows and eyelashes until you don't have them, and specks of dust feel like sandpaper on your eyeballs. I was fortunate in that I experienced almost no nausea but had terrible mouth sores that prevented me from eating and sometimes even speaking. The worst part, though, was the chemo brain. As a straight-A student, I found it crushing to withdraw from school soon after my initial chemo dose. I couldn't concentrate and my eyes would dart all over the room. I was anemic, lethargic, and prone to fainting. It felt as if my body was trying to kill me. It was the toughest psychological ordeal I have ever gone through, but thinking of Terry and his bravery fuelled me to stay positive. "Mind over body" became my mantra and continues to be to this day.

After three rounds of chemo, it was time for the operation. My surgeon said, "Anna, you have a fifty-fifty chance of waking up with your toes. I'll do what I can to save your leg, but it's possible you'll wake up without it." When I woke up, all I cared about was seeing my toes. And they were there! All ten piggies still intact. I had never been so grateful in my life. Little did I know that the hard part was just beginning.

After completing three more chemotherapy rounds, I returned to school and managed to graduate alongside my peers that June. I had big plans for my future and refused to let cancer stand in the way! Except for the short hair, unrelenting pain in my right leg, and continued reliance on crutches, all was well.

Then one day a little over a year since the initial surgery, my scar split open and pus started oozing out. I was rushed to the hospital for emergency surgery; my persistent pain and limited mobility were due to a massive but discreet infection I had developed soon after the initial operation. Months of IV antibiotics followed and another surgery was performed later that year to replace the loosened medley of metal and plastic parts that held my upper and lower leg together. I was once again fortunate enough to wake up with all ten toes and begin the slow process of learning how to walk again, having spent two-and-a-half years on crutches. Within a few months, I was walking somewhat independently, and soon after I only thought about cancer during my quarterly checkups.

But my world came crashing down a second time when, at age twenty, I was told the cancer had spread to my left lung. My first thought was, "This is it. This is how Terry died and this is how I will die."

Despite tremendous love and support from my family and boyfriend, I felt scared, lost, and helpless. Facing the very real possibility that I could die, I wanted to fight back directly, not just by swallowing pills, agreeing to surgeries, and accepting IV drugs. I wanted to make a difference. I reached out to Terry's younger brother, Darrell, who was the national director of the Terry Fox Foundation at the time. He responded right away, saying my message brought tears to his eyes, and invited me to be a Terry's Team Member. A Terry's Team Member is a supporter of the foundation who has a personal diagnosis of cancer, is at any stage of their treatment or recovery, and participates in the Terry Fox Run. That summer, before going in for lung surgery, I did a CTV interview to celebrate the twenty-fifth anniversary of Terry's Marathon of Hope. A few weeks later, I had my fourth operation in less than three years. The surgeon removed the whole lower lobe and two wedges from the upper lobe of my left lung. I went home a few days later and watched the interview on TV, feeling so incredibly grateful to Terry.

In September 2005, I attended my very first Burnaby Terry Fox Run and then underwent six months of elective chemotherapy to ensure, as much as possible, that all the cancer cells were gone. Once my strength returned, I joined the Burnaby Terry Fox Run organizing committee and eventually took on the run organizer role, getting all my family and friends involved. Every September, I speak at various schools about my and Terry's stories and why it's so important to keep his legacy alive. I fundraise and act as a spokesperson for the foundation as much as possible. I am proof positive that cancer research works.

I try not to think of my cancer journey very often anymore, unless it's Terry Fox Run season or time for a tune-up (parts of my knee implant need to be replaced every ten to fifteen years). But when I do sit quietly and take stock of what I've been through, it's impossible not to credit everything to Terry. He is my personal saviour. I wholeheartedly believe that were it not for him and his Marathon of Hope, I would have lost my leg and my life.

Terry sacrificed his life so that people like me could live. I think of him every day and say a silent thank you each morning as I get out bed and look at my toes. I don't know if I'll ever be able to repay the tremendous debt I owe to Terry Fox, but I hope that he'd be proud of the way I share our stories with the world to keep his message of hope alive.

Steeling himself for every step, and changing the world as he did.

Hayley Wickenheiser

LONG REVERED AS the best female hockey player of all time, Hayley Wickenheiser is a titan of sport and a leader both on and off the ice. As a member of Canada's national women's team for twenty-three years, she helped earn her country four Olympic gold medals and seven World Championships. Currently, Hayley is assistant director of player development for the Toronto Maple Leafs and is pursuing a medical degree.

As an athlete, I've always been in awe of Terry Fox's mental resiliency. Forget about the physicality of what he did—which is amazing in itself—but his ability to endure physical and emotional pain to a level that most people couldn't endure for even an hour puts everything into perspective. What's a punishing gym workout in comparison, or a gruelling bike ride? When I was suffering through long training sessions, I would often find a place to focus, to go somewhere else in my mind. It seemed Terry had that ability times 100. He tended to look straight ahead and slightly down ahead of him. With every step that he took, I think he was steeling his body but he was also steeling his mind. Terry pushed past limits that most of us would find daunting on our best days. In doing so, he inspired us all.

Although I was too young to witness his Marathon of
Hope, I first learned about Terry from my schoolteachers in
Shaunavon, Saskatchewan, and from my parents, also teach-
ers, who believed physical activity was important and powerful. They were all passionate about Terry's story and made sure
we understood the significance of what he'd accomplished.
Every September, my friends and I would bike around town
to raise money, and then we'd do the run together. I took part
in the run off and on throughout my teen years, too. When I
think of Terry Fox, I recall those memories, but more than
anything else, I envision one photo of him. I believe he was
somewhere in Ontario, and he was running through the
rain wearing just his white T-shirt, grey shorts, and Adidas
runners. I remember seeing that picture for the first time and
thinking, "Wow, running across Canada. That's a lot."

Terry is one of the most influential Canadians in our history. Because we need to know where we come from in order
to know where we're going, I'm thrilled that younger generations still learn about Terry Fox—my own family included.
I recently had a conversation with my five-year-old niece:
she'd heard about the Terry Fox Run and thought it was a
fundraiser to save foxes. It was so sweet and innocent, but my
sister explained the real meaning to her. The next day, I asked
her what she had learned and she said, "The Terry Fox Run is
to help people with cancer." Then she ran around the play-
ground to raise a bit of money for her first run. While I don't
think kids need to know all about the tragedies of cancer, I
do believe they should know people can get sick and we do

everything we can to help them. And what Terry did for cancer is unmatchable, in my opinion. He set the stage for millions of dollars to be raised and created unbelievable awareness. People with much more obscure illnesses would give anything to have a Terry Fox advocating on their behalf.

Now that I'm studying medicine and dealing with patients of my own, Terry's memory serves as a beacon of hope, a reminder that anything is possible. We like to try to predict the future, but we don't always know what people are capable of. Terry taught me to never underestimate the power of the human spirit. Whenever I see the statue of him that stands in Victoria, B.C., I reflect on his resiliency, compassion, and courage. Terry was a Canadian hero, one of the greatest ever, and it's important that we never forget him. Participating in the Terry Fox Run is such a good way to keep his memory alive and to keep up the fight against cancer. But I think we can honour him in our day-to-day lives, too, by striving to do the best we can, always, and rising above any challenge we might face. By giving our best every day, we can all embody the spirit of Terry Fox.

From my very first fundraiser, people have never failed to come out and support Terry's dream. As Terry showed us, we can accomplish a lot alone, but together, we can change the world.

Jocelyn Adams

JOCELYN ADAMS IS a grade nine student in Tecumseh, Ontario. She has been fundraising for the Terry Fox Foundation since she was nearly four years old, as seen in her photo.

"I want to try the impossible to show that it can be done." This quote by Terry Fox reminds me of the incredible perseverance and determination that he had. His strength has always been such an inspiration to me.

When I was almost four years old, our family was preparing to do the Terry Fox Run in our town of Tecumseh, Ontario. The night before the run, my parents showed me a video about Terry so that I could understand who he was and what his Marathon of Hope was all about. The next day at the event, I asked them why we were donating money and they said, "It's going to help people with cancer." I was so young, but that really stuck with me. Later that night, my parents found me standing out on our porch, trying to sell our leftover pizza. When they asked what I was doing, I simply shrugged at my mom and said, "I'm raising money for Terry Fox." My mom told me that I couldn't sell our leftovers but asked me what I wanted to sell. We had some granola bars and apples so she helped me set up a table to sell those instead. She called a few of her friends and asked them to stop by to support me.

I didn't make much money that night and I'm sure my parents thought I'd soon forget all about the fundraising, but when my mom picked me up from junior kindergarten the next day, the first thing I asked her was, "Am I going to sell again tonight?" There was no way that she could turn me down. We decided that cookies would sell better than granola bars so we picked some up and set up a stand with cookies, apples, and water. This went on every night for about two weeks, and my parents created an online dona-tion page for me to raise funds as well. By the time our school's Terry Fox Run rolled around a few weeks later, I'd raised $700.

The following summer, my parents took me to some yard sales and that's when my ideas about fundraising started to change. I asked my parents if I could fundraise for Terry again this year but this time by having a yard sale. That initial sale ended up being such a success that we decided to make it an annual event.

We started out small, collecting a few donations from my parents' friends and co-workers. Now when we host the sale, we start gathering items as early as July and we keep them in a large storage bin that a local company donates. The bin sits on our driveway for the six weeks leading up to the sale. Even with that, we still can't use our garage for the entire month of August—that's how much stuff our community donates. Setting up for the sale is a huge team effort. We always hold it on the first Saturday after Labour Day, and I recruit my family, friends, and my Taekwon-Do teammates to help us get ready. Even with a crew this size, it still takes about four hours to spread the items out over our property and the properties of several neigh-bours. People donate everything from sports equipment and

electronics to gas fireplaces and furniture. I feel honoured that
people choose to donate their items for our sale, instead of
selling them elsewhere to make money for themselves. We don't
price a single thing: we accept fair donations and I am always
astonished by the generosity of people. Sometimes complete
strangers will buy very small items yet leave large donations
because they believe so strongly in the cause. I'm so grateful to
all of the people who have donated their time, goods, and money
to our yard sales; we truly could not do it without them.

Over the past ten years, through both our yard sales and
the online donation page, we've raised more than $30,000 for
the Terry Fox Foundation. As I get older, I want to continue to
fundraise for the foundation and maybe even come up with
some new ideas to raise money. Anything we can do to help
Terry's cause is worth it. His example inspired me from a
young age to help others, and so has his family. I am in awe of
the fact that they have dedicated their entire lives to keeping
Terry's dream alive. I have had some family members affected
by cancer so that also motivates me to continue. I want to be a
part of eventually finding a cure for cancer.

If my experience in fundraising has taught me anything, it's
that when a community comes together we can make a huge
impact. Thanks to the very generous people in my community,
we're able to raise awareness and money to help fight cancer. I
believe that every dollar counts. Terry said, "Even if I don't finish, we need others to continue. It's got to keep going without
me." My hope is that all young people find a way to get involved
and support Terry's dream. Together we can make a difference.

*The running that transformed a nation, forever immortalized in bronze,
Terry Fox Plaza, Vancouver, B.C.*

Douglas Coupland

DOUGLAS COUPLAND IS a Canadian novelist and artist. Since 1991, he has written thirteen novels, written and performed for the Royal Shakespeare Company, and has had his art displayed in museums around the world. He is the author of *Terry*, published in 2005 by Douglas & McIntyre, and is the creator of the Terry Fox Memorial in Vancouver, B.C.

———————————

Bronze statues are unusual in that if you made a bronze of someone that's exactly life-sized, even of a basketball player, people will walk up to it and say, "Boy, they sure were tiny in real life." In order for a bronze to look statuesque, it needs to be, at the very least, about 125 percent life-sized.

I didn't realize this until the day in 2010 when we (myself and Grout McTavish Architects) installed the Terry Fox Memorial at the intersection of Robson and Beatty Streets in Vancouver. For those who haven't seen it, the work is comprised of four statues of Terry in poses which, if strung together, make an animation loop of Terry's distinct running style that we came to know during the 1980 Marathon of Hope. The first Terry is exactly life-sized, and the fourth Terry is twice life-sized. My thinking was that if the work was to be dug up in a thousand years, whoever dug it up would be able to figure out what's going on there. And the fact that the Terry figures get bigger might convey the notion of something growing as it pushes forward.

I think the day we installed the work was also the day human beings discovered selfies, and the life-sized Terry became Selfie Central. If you go online, there are thousands and thousands of photos of people standing with Terry, and when I speak with people there on the plaza (I visit a few times a year), many say, "I didn't realize he was that short." I point out that he's actually tall—it's just the trick of bronze that shrinks one's perception of scale. Then they say, "Oh yeah, you're right." But I think this misperception is actually a great thing because it makes Terry feel incredibly approachable and familiar, which he is in the minds of so many people. I sometimes wonder what the effect would have been if I had made a forty-foot-tall Terry painted black with laser beams shooting from his eyes. It probably wouldn't have felt so approachable.

Time moves on. Terry's run ended September 1, 1980, the day before I started art school, and I remember hearing the news on the car radio as I was preparing for that first day. That was forty years ago. OMG: *forty*. Has the world changed in forty years? Of course, and I think it's almost entirely for the better—I'm an optimist.

I'm writing this on a Boeing 787-9 currently over Alberta. Over the wifi, I'm streaming all sorts of images and archival film footage of Terry. If I wanted to, here in my seat, I could have the answer to almost any question delivered to me instantaneously and for free, with no judgment. I could watch pretty much any film or TV show ever made. You get the point: we humans take things for granted. I mention this because one thing we all now take for granted is the legacy of Terry's run. I remember growing up when cancer was a scary boogey-man. You couldn't even whisper the word or you'd jinx things. Also, back then, people with disabilities were hidden away. Literally. People kept them hidden. Wheelchairs meant shame and impending death. Nobody talked about anything. It was actually really creepy. Terry blew up the walls around cancer and disability. He was the kid next door who suddenly brought sunlight into darkness and banished the boogeyman forever. What an astonishing gift to the world.

I would like to tell you of one perhaps unique moment I had with Terry's legacy. It was sixteen years ago, and I was preparing to write a book on him. My research began with a portion of the Fox family's archive materials, which at that time were stored in a freezing-cold cinder-block room inside Vancouver's BC Place stadium. There were hundreds of boxes and piles, and it was truly overwhelming. I had no idea where to begin. One thing I did quickly learn, though, was that pretty much every mother in Canada had written a letter to Terry. Maybe you didn't know it, but they did. Many of the letters were written in greeting cards, hundreds of thousands of them, and all of these cards and letters had that same hand-writing that everyone's mother used to have. I remember reading one card out of thousands, and something strange happened—the world fell away from me and I was magically just standing there in space and surrounding me was this constellation of lights, the wishes of hope and love from every mother in the country, and I felt safer and happier there in that freezing room than perhaps anywhere else in my life.

I'm now above Saskatchewan. If I wanted to, I could edit a movie on my laptop or take a virtual trip to the hidden caves of Antarctica or learn how to program my kitchen micro-wave or . . . or maybe I could just sit here and look out at the prairies and marvel at what a beautiful world we live in—and give thanks that people like Terry exist and they cancel out our badness and return us to a finer state of being.

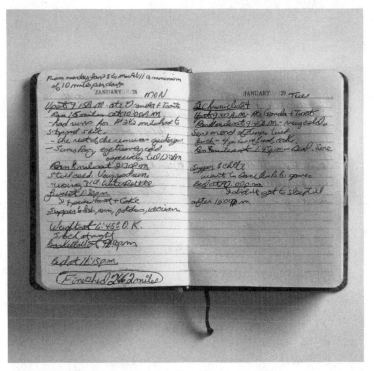

Terry's training journal.

Having the Terry Fox Award in my office is a daily reminder of Terry's strength, courage, and determination—every day, it inspires me to work toward a better future.

John Kearsey

JOHN KEARSEY GREW up in St. John's, Newfoundland, where Terry began his Marathon of Hope. John is the vice-president of external relations at the University of Manitoba, where he creates opportunities for people to support education, health, and culture through philanthropy. He is the 2019–20 chair of the Terry Fox Humanitarian Award, which he received in 1985.

In 1980, I was a thirteen-year-old in need of someone to look up to, for many different reasons. The Six Million Dollar Man and the Bionic Woman were my heroes from TV shows, but I was old enough to know they weren't real. Who were the real heroes out there?

When I caught my first glimpse of Terry Fox on the evening news as he began his cross-Canada trek in my hometown of St. John's, he caught my attention like no other public figure ever had. This beautiful, young man with his flowing curls, genuine smile, and focused eyes was one of us and yet something more. There was a purity in his sense of purpose. His every pained but determined step opened up a space for us all to support and cheer him with hope and without judgment. Everybody was welcome, needed, moved. For me, at that time, with my heart and my dreams and my questions, it meant the world.

I had found my real hero.

I followed Terry's journey, reading, watching, or listening to as much coverage as I could. A marathon every day. I didn't really know what that meant at the time. I particularly loved when he kept adding province names to his T-shirt. I hated seeing blood stains on his shorts. I loved when he smiled at supporters cheering him on from the roadside. I hated seeing pain in his face.

But before long, Terry was on a gurney being wheeled from a plane. "Somewhere," he said in a short interview, "the hurting must stop." I think that moment ignited a passion in the entire country: now *everyone* was paying attention. I didn't dare leave the house the day Lloyd Robertson hosted the national telethon to support Terry's vision of one dollar from every Canadian; I wanted to track every second of it.

Months passed. My passion for Terry Fox's Marathon of Hope only intensified. Then one Sunday in early summer 1981, I was on the way to Mass where I volunteered as an altar server, and the news came on the radio. Terry had died. At church, I asked to have a prayer read out for Terry. To hide my tears, I kept my head down. After all, I didn't *know* Terry. Why was I so emotional? But when the reader paused in the middle of pronouncing Terry's name, I couldn't resist looking around. There were hundreds of tears in the church that morning. We knew we had lost someone special. Someone we cherished. Gone. Those eyes, that smile, that posture—all etched in our memories. And in our hearts was something eternal, whether we realized it in that moment or not.

The need to follow Terry's example had taken root: to give, to help, to care. Inspired by Terry and the loss of my uncle and grandmother to cancer, I volunteered at a palliative care unit, helping families as their loved ones passed from this world to the next. I got involved organizing the Terry Fox Run, which was a pretty small event in St. John's during its early days. What fun it was working with great pals who were also highly committed to Terry's legacy. The St. John's run almost tripled in size in three years. That, and later—during my first couple of years at university—being part of the provincial board of directors, allowed me to be among the thousands of Canadians committed to keeping Terry's dream alive.

In 1985, I received a phone call that changed my entire life. The voice on the line told me I had been selected as a recipient of the Terry Fox Humanitarian Award, one of fifty in Canada that year. I was floored. These scholarships are given annually to graduating students who have demonstrated humanitarian service while in pursuit of excellence in academics, amateur sport, fitness, health, or community service. They allow young Canadians to continue striving to live by the ideals Terry did, through the pursuit of higher education. The financial aspect of the award was the equivalent of a million dollars to me. My family didn't have two dimes to support my education. I was determined to attend university; I would be the first in my family to do so. I dreamed of becoming a social worker to help families work through death and dying. My time at the palliative care unit, my personal experiences of grief, and Terry's light guided this goal. But this award was about more to me than money. I wasn't a straight-A student. I grew up feeling inferior in many ways, and this affected my ability to ace high school. The Terry Fox Award was a vote of confidence like nothing I'd ever felt. And off to university I went. While I didn't end up in social work, I did go on to build a career in health and education, connecting committed donors with opportunities to create brighter futures for communities. If it wasn't for Terry, I'm not sure I would have been inspired to volunteer, to push past obstacles, and to be gentle on myself when I didn't reach my original goals.

Today, I'm the chair of the Terry Fox Humanitarian Award program and we continue to honour Terry's determination by recognizing young Canadians for their humanitarianism and for overcoming challenges in the pursuit of excellence. It's our hope that this encourages young people to follow in Terry's footsteps. To make a difference in our society. The award carries on Terry's dream. We all have the opportunity to emulate Terry's humanitarian contribution, his selflessness and humility, and that is the path to a better future.

Someone once said to me that it's too bad Terry wasn't able to finish. I replied, "On the contrary, Terry has never stopped."

The sock Terry wore on the foot of his artificial leg for the duration of the Marathon of Hope.

Me with the man who proved his ability to the world, and improved it beyond measure.

Rick Hansen

RICK HANSEN IS the founder of the Rick Hansen Foundation and a passionate supporter of people with disabilities in Canada and around the world. Rick is best known as the "Man in Motion" for his epic twenty-six-month, thirty-four-country, 40,000-kilometre global wheelchair trip to make the world inclusive for people with disabilities and to find a cure for paralysis.

One evening many years ago, I was having dinner with some friends. They were chatting about a young man who used to play basketball for Simon Fraser University and had recently lost his leg to cancer. I was a member of the Vancouver Cable Cars wheelchair basketball team, and our manager and mentor, Stan Stronge, was always encouraging us to recruit new athletes. I got the name and number of the guy and called him out of the blue. It was, of course, Terry. I described the sport and our team to him and then asked him to consider joining one of our practices. He was super excited and positive. We hit it off right away, and he said he'd come out to join us the very next week.

I was waiting on the sidelines for Terry to show up, and when he did, I noticed he was walking fairly gingerly with his artificial leg. It was all so new to him still. We brought a wheelchair for him to sit in, and you could see right away he had a willingness to learn. He was very keen on basketball, and although he was weak from chemotherapy, he showed how determined he was. It was an exciting and inspiring first meeting. As I got to know Terry, I found that we had a lot in common. I was just a year and a bit older than him; he was studying kinesiology at Simon Fraser University while I was studying physical education at the University of British Columbia. We were both committed to our sport and we shared so many of the same values, having grown up in similar middle-class families. We became good friends and ended up training together, outside of our team practices.

Terry and I were always trying to develop our skills and push our endurance, which is a key component of wheelchair basketball—you really need stamina to perform at a high level. So, Terry started pushing up a hill near Simon Fraser University, and I would join him when I could get over there from UBC. We'd meet at the bottom, park our cars, and then wheel all the way up along the side of the highway. It was quite a few kilometres up a fairly steep mountain. Once we got to the top, we'd go to the university to do weights and shoot hoops. Then we'd glide back down to our cars—through cold and rain—and go our separate ways. Eventually, we learned to leave one car at the top! We spent a lot of time together—as much as our different university schedules would allow—and really bonded. Terry didn't stop this training when he didn't have a workout buddy, though; often, he would be pushing up that hill solo. I developed a tremendous amount of respect for Terry as a human being and as a friend.

Being immersed in the team inspired Terry. He became comfortable with his "disability" and saw more of his ability. I think that really liberated him. Terry was driven and had a real interest in going as far as he could in sport. On one of our drives home from a game in Portland, we had been chatting about everything under the sun, but when the conversation paused, I could tell he was pondering something important. Then he said, "So Rick, I've been thinking about doing something and I wanted to ask your opinion." I asked, "Sure, what is it?" He said, "Well, I'm thinking about running across the country with the purpose of raising money for cancer research. What do you think?" And I said, "Wow. That's really inspiring. That's really amazing." He asked if I thought he could do it. There was no question: I had no doubt in my mind he could make it. I was honoured to be among the first to hear about his dream.

When Terry started his Marathon of Hope, it was difficult to stay in touch, but we got updates from his family and from Stan. It was pretty special to see the progression; in the early days, we didn't hear much in the media but then everything started to build and soon we saw his journey covered nationwide. I was so happy for him and so inspired. Sadly, we all know what happened. We received the shocking news, and the next thing I knew, Terry was back in Vancouver to get treatments at the hospital. We hung out together, as best we could, and Terry's mindset was strong. He said, "I'm sidelined for the moment, but I'm going to beat this thing again. If I can, I'll get back out there and finish the run." Terry had become a bit of a celebrity, but through it all, he stayed so grounded and modest. He didn't understand what all the fuss was about. Terry was such a good guy, and it was a privilege to be there with him, his friends, and his family toward the end.

I miss Terry, and our society suffered a great loss when he passed away. But he left us so much. Terry was an ordinary Canadian with extraordinary determination and a passion to make a difference. He had something in him that we all have within ourselves: hope. We all have the ability to move the bar a little farther, a little higher. It just takes courage. Terry had the courage to try, to cut through fear, self-doubt, and cynicism and take that first step. He dipped his artificial leg in the Atlantic Ocean and turned westward. It was an uncertain journey and it didn't manifest to the end, but just look at the impact he had and the legacy he created.

Terry showed everyone that people with disabilities have ability, and his journey inspired me to embark on my Man in Motion World Tour. I, too, wanted to raise awareness about the potential of people with disabilities, and I wouldn't have done it if not for his friendship. Terry's parents were there when I left Oakridge Mall in Vancouver on March 21, 1985. They gave me a miniature replica of the statue of Terry in Thunder Bay. I took it with me all around the world. At times when I thought I couldn't keep going, it gave me incredible inspiration. Just like when we were in practices together or pushing ourselves up that mountain, Terry encouraged and challenged me.

So, I hope when people think about Terry, they realize there's a little bit of him in all of us, because we *all* have ability.

A rare photo of Terry playing volleyball, within a year of the surgery to remove his right leg.

In the Terry Fox Laboratory, 1990—the place where so many innovations have been discovered. A place that would not have existed without Terry.

Connie and Allen Eaves

CONNIE AND ALLEN Eaves co-founded the Terry Fox Laboratory in 1981 at the BC Cancer Agency. Since then, this award-winning couple has made significant strides in understanding normal blood stem cells and how disruptions can lead to cancer initiation and progression. Today, Connie continues to serve as a distinguished scientist at the Terry Fox Laboratory and as a professor of medical genetics at the University of British Columbia, while Allen is president and CEO of STEMCELL Technologies, Canada's largest biotechnology company.

When it comes to finding a cure for cancer, we have always wanted to help and to feel the excitement of being a part of medical history. It's a complicated endeavour, and it requires input from many diverse perspectives. There's room for everybody—and we are very proud to be part of that everybody.

Early in our careers in the 1970s, we had decided that the only way to cure cancer was through research. We advocated for the creation of a leukemia research group in British Columbia; there wasn't a lot happening in the province at the time in that field. Then in the middle of Terry's run in 1980, the Ontario and B.C. governments each announced $1 million

donations to cancer research based in the respective provinces. We were asked to do something meaningful with the
B.C. money, and this is what led to the creation of the Terry
Fox Laboratory, officially born in 1981 with a total group of
twenty-six people. Today, the Terry Fox Laboratory consists of
close to 150 scientists, trainees, and support staff. Everything
that we've accomplished along the way is thanks to Terry. He
took that first step (literally) and initiated a marathon of cancer research that continues to evolve and have an impact today.

One of our most significant advances was made during the
lab's early years. We were trying to understand the abnormal
growth that causes chronic myeloid leukemia by investigating
such growth in tissue culture. It turned out that the leukemic
cells wouldn't grow outside of the body and, seemingly out
of the blue, normal blood cells started to appear. This discovery, published in the *New England Journal of Medicine* in
1983, was important for two reasons. First, it showed that a
large population of normal blood stem cells is still present in
most patients with chronic myeloid leukemia, even though
the cells had not been previously detectable. This amazing
advance prompted a global search for even better approaches
to eliminate the disease, some of which have now led to cures.
Second, this early observation also suggested that normal
blood stem cells can be kept alive at least for a few days outside the body, thus laying the foundation for successful gene
therapy strategies now being developed to cure patients with
many types of diseases. However, it turns out that chronic
myeloid leukemia is among the simplest cancers to treat.

Translating its treatment approaches to many other cancers has been difficult and slow.

What *is* revolutionizing outcomes for patients? Sophisticated ways of detecting mutations have led to some major advances, particularly in cancers that are diagnosed at a very early stage. Unfortunately, most cancers are not diagnosed early. Research on every aspect of what cancer actually is and how it develops is therefore still extraordinarily important. We need to understand basic cell alterations, develop new methods to detect them, and find new ways to test how promising therapies will work in patients. This is why we need the Terry Fox Run and the Terry Fox Foundation. People need to be inspired to donate so that researchers across Canada have the resources required to find answers to the many questions that remain.

We met Terry only once—but our brief exchange has stuck with us all these years. He was a very modest, personable, and sensitive individual, with a clear vision of how he wanted to see improvements in cancer treatment made through research. We met him after the Marathon of Hope had ended; at the time, we didn't fully appreciate how much work Terry had done investigating how research was best supported. He was passionate that funding should be given without bias, based solely on advancing science. We could see he was a perceptive young man who was determined to do his best to make things better in a thoughtful, measured way. He certainly has. His influence on the world of cancer research has been profound. Thanks to the lab and the funding we've received since its inception, we've been able to supervise the training of more than 100 scientists, many of whom have gone on to pursue cancer research across Canada and around the world.

Every day, the scientific community comes closer to a cure. We now have tools to analyze the trillions of cells present in a human body. Today, research is focused on measuring those cells and their millions of different molecular components that determine how they move, divide, or become malignant. We don't know how soon we'll be able to fully understand these processes because of their complexity. There are many aspects of biology that we believe are close to being understood, but most are much more complicated than we ever envisaged. Fortunately, we can now use incredibly powerful tools to address this challenge, and we expect to change how cancer is diagnosed, treated, and ultimately even prevented. We are on the verge of a much greater understanding of life itself. It is hard to predict what the first outcomes of that will be, but we know they will be exciting.

We aren't young scientists anymore, but we are committed to supporting the global scientific community as we all seek cures. Terry remains an inspiration. To us, he has always represented the hope of youth, of seeing no barriers. Young people just want to go out and make good things happen. We may be older now, but we still feel that way, because of Terry.

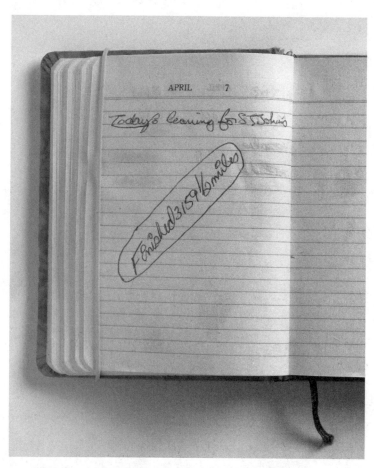

APRIL 7

Today's leaving for S.S.Johns

Finished 3159½ miles

Terry's training journal, the day he left home to start his marathon. It took Terry and Doug two days to fly across the country, touching down in 10 cities and 9 of the 10 provinces.

Terry Fox and Isadore Sharp at a Four Seasons luncheon hosted for Terry in Toronto (July 1980).

Isadore Sharp

ISADORE SHARP IS the founder and chairman of Four Seasons Hotels and Resorts, the world's leading luxury hospitality company, which he founded in 1960. Today, Four Seasons operates 117 hotels and resorts, as well as forty-five residences, in forty-seven countries worldwide. Isadore founded the annual Terry Fox Run, and is also the chair emeritus of the Terry Fox Foundation.

It is said that once you are personally affected by cancer, you become more sensitive to it, more aware of its ability to touch people across all backgrounds and cultures. This was certainly the case for my family, having lost our teenage son to cancer two years before we learned of a young man running across Canada for cancer research. We all know now that this young man was Terry Fox, a Canadian icon and hero for many. But at the time, he was an unknown, driven by a fiery passion few ever possess, facing an uncertain future and seemingly skeptical world.

Hearing about his journey from afar, my family and I felt immediately that we wanted to, needed to, help him on his journey. At first, I was surprised by how few people were paying attention and how many dismissed his run as a gimmick.

And so we created a program at Four Seasons that pledged two dollars for every mile that he ran. We took out ads in major newspapers across Canada calling on 999 other business leaders to join Four Seasons, doing our small part to raise awareness of this incredible young man. After we took out the ads, Terry—from a pay phone on the side of the road—called me directly, having heard about what we had done. It was the first of many conversations between us, and he let me know how moved he was by our pledge, that he had been ready to throw in the towel, but that our care and commitment inspired him to continue.

Throughout his run, as Terry completed an astounding full marathon each day, even as his body threw obstacles in his way, his Marathon of Hope became ours. In communities large and small, Terry was greeted by cheering crowds, joined by other runners, met by schoolchildren who had saved their pennies to donate, all while receiving the heartfelt encouragement of those who had been touched by cancer themselves.

Terry spoke at a luncheon in Toronto that we hosted in his honour. Unscripted, wearing just a T-shirt and shorts, he addressed a roomful of business leaders who sat gazing up at Terry in complete and utter awe. I clearly remember he was flipping a paperclip while he spoke; the room was so unbelievably silent as we were all transfixed by his story, the flicking of the paperclip slightly echoing around us. In his calm, authentic, and genuine manner, Terry spoke of his journey and his call to action, profoundly inspiring us to help him spread his message as he continued to run across Canada.

And he did keep running. Even when he was forced to abandon his marathon, he insisted that he would keep going, somehow, just as soon as he recovered. But understanding he was unlikely to run again as his cancer spread, I sent Terry the following telegram to ensure he knew how dedicated we were to him:

Dear Terry,

The Marathon of Hope has just begun. You started it. We will not rest until your dream to find a cure for cancer is realized.

I am asking every Four Seasons hotel to organize, along with the local branches of the Cancer Society, a Terry Fox Marathon of Hope Run to be held on the first Sunday of October. Beginning this year, it will become an annual fundraising event for the Terry Fox Cancer Research Fund and we will not stop until cancer has been beaten.

We will also ask every city and town across Canada to join in on the same day so that you will be running in our hearts and minds every year until the battle is won.

Your courage and determination is an inspiration to us all. Our hearts and prayers are with you.

With deep admiration and affection,
Isadore Sharp
(September 1980)

Shortly after I sent the telegram, I spoke with Terry to see how he was doing, and we further discussed the idea of an annual fundraising run. He liked the idea but insisted that it should be voluntary, non-competitive, and open to anyone. By February 1981, as momentum and attention grew, Terry's story continued to inspire fundraising. Eventually, he surpassed his goal of $24 million, which was, at the time, equivalent to one dollar for every Canadian. Shortly after this call, we set the plans in motion.

While he did not survive to see the first Terry Fox Run a year later, his wishes were respected, as they have been at every Terry Fox Run across Canada and around the world over the past four decades, in what has become the largest single-day fundraiser for cancer research, contributing close to $800 million to the cause that fired his spirit and inspired a nation.

That first year, the inaugural Terry Fox Run was held in more than 700 locations across Canada, including one in Toronto organized by Four Seasons. Every year since then, hundreds of Four Seasons employees and their families volunteer their time to organize this annual Terry Fox Run at Wilket Creek Park and are joined by thousands of people, often participating as families and embracing Terry's cause together as they run, walk, and ride. The Terry Fox Run at Wilket Creek Park alone has raised more than $11 million.

Since those early days of the Terry Fox Run, the population of Canada has increased by more than 50 percent, and new Canadians are joining the movement, too. Perhaps they first learned the story of this brave young Canadian at a run held in Seattle or Singapore, Buenos Aires or Bangkok, and perhaps they have their own personal stories of how cancer has affected them.

Terry will always be a part of the history of not only Canada but also humanity. It was an honour and privilege to know him and to be a part of his brave and hopeful marathon. As I committed to Terry four decades ago, I will not rest until his dream is realized and we will not stop running until the battle is won.

Terry's example taught us to be bigger than ourselves and push through difficult times to make a difference for others.

Perdita Felicien

PERDITA FELICIEN IS a World Champion hurdler, sports broadcaster, and author of *My Mother's Daughter*, her forthcoming memoir to be published by Doubleday Canada in March 2021. She competed at the 2000 and 2004 Summer Olympics; was the first Canadian woman in track and field to win gold at the World Championships; and in 2004, set the Canadian record in the 100-metres hurdles with a time of 12.46 seconds. Perdita lives in Toronto, Ontario, with her husband and daughter.

What makes Terry Fox remarkable is that he was an everyday Canadian, an ordinary kid, who decided to give voice to the fight against cancer. There wasn't a lot of fanfare when he first declared he was going to run across the country. But as he started to move west, Canadians paid attention. What touched a lot of people, and what touches me now when I think about him, is the example he showed us that any one of us can make a change. We can all take up a cause in our own lives, in our hometowns, and we can channel Terry's energy to do good. You don't have to be a humanitarian or an activist to make a difference in your community. That's why I respect Terry Fox so much. He wasn't a millionaire. He wasn't a movie star. He was a guy who loved sport, was diagnosed with cancer, and set out to raise one dollar from every Canadian.

I don't think any of us can truly appreciate how gruelling
it must have been to run a marathon every day for months.
Terry's spirit was magnificent. When I learned that he kept
a journal during the Marathon of Hope, I imagined it as an
outlet, a safe place for him to keep his hopes, his pain, his
dreams, and his frustrations. I've kept journals ever since I
was young, even while I was competing at Olympic Games.
Writing in them has been my way to relieve pent-up emotions.
Terry was not at an Olympic starting line, but he was running
a tremendous race, a race with its own heaviness, anxiety,
and doubt. Getting my feelings down on the page relieves me;
I don't have to carry them anymore because I've given them
a tangible place to dwell. Journals are also a place for your
hope and excitement to live. I would imagine Terry went back
to read his words, to see what got him through day three or
day six. I hope that uplifted him when he felt overwhelmed.

As a new mother, now when I think of the people who
loved him, I realize how selfless his parents were. To deal
with Terry's diagnosis would have been devastating, in the
first place. To then support him as he set out on a very public,
cross-country journey would not have been easy. Their
instincts would likely have been to keep him sheltered in
their house, to care for him and keep him close. I can only
imagine how they felt. Before having my baby girl, Nova, I
was only responsible for myself. Now, the knowledge that
there's someone else in the world that I care so much about is
both amazing and frightening. Parenthood, I'm learning, is
a beautiful act of letting go, of helping someone pursue their

own path. I admire Terry's family for empowering him to follow his dream—and for sharing him with all of us.

I can't pinpoint the exact moment in elementary school when I learned about Terry, but I can vividly recall the year he helped me through one of my lowest times ever. I was heading into 2008 as one of the top two hurdlers in the world, having run one of my fastest times at the 2007 World Championships, and I was feeling hopeful about the 2008 Summer Olympics. Then I got injured. I was forced to miss the Games and I was devastated, especially since I'd waited four years to redeem myself after crashing out at the 2004 Olympics. I'd just come back from Beijing in August 2008 when the organizers of the Terry Fox Run in Pickering, my hometown, asked if I'd participate. I was licking my wounds and did not feel like going. Eventually, I thought to myself, "Hold on a minute. Terry Fox was dealt a much tougher blow and did not feel sorry for himself." I decided to support the run, to honour and celebrate this great Canadian. When I went back to my training base in Illinois a few weeks after that experience, I understood that we all face bad days. How we deal with them is up to us.

Everyone has a story, and everyone's circumstances are different, but I was taught that we all have the ability to steer our lives toward a brighter horizon. And we don't know where that might take us, but we go toward it anyway. It seems to me that as Terry was going west, that's really what he wanted to do. He didn't make it to British Columbia. He didn't get as far as he wanted to go. But I feel like we are all moving west in Terry's honour.

The van that has seen so much; my family snapped a photo with Darrell Fox after a run celebrating the 28th anniversary of the Marathon of Hope in 2008.

Craig Jarvis

CRAIG JARVIS IS a manager and wealth adviser at Scotia-McLeod in Toronto. He, his wife Judy, and their children Nolan, Windemere, and Somerset are passionate about supporting the Terry Fox Foundation, among other charitable organizations.

A roaring fire was keeping guests warm inside a large teepee in the mountains of Banff National Park. My colleagues had gathered for a fundraising auction in support of the Terry Fox Foundation in early 2007, and we were so fortunate to have Darrell Fox as our speaker. When Terry's younger brother entered the room, you could hear a pin drop. Needing no introduction, Darrell graciously and passionately shared stories from the Marathon of Hope and about the challenges Terry had faced. Twenty-seven years after Terry's historic run, Darrell brought the room to tears with his emotional words.

As the chair of that evening's fundraiser, my job hosting the live auction was made considerably easier after Darrell's dynamic speech. There was no need for me to remind folks of the important cause we were raising money for. I'm usually calm and collected, and have no issues with public speaking, but that evening I found myself choked up. Standing beside Darrell and listening to his account of Terry's surgery and horrific chemo treatment brought me back to my own battle with aggressive bladder cancer three years earlier. As a healthy forty-three-year-old father of three, I was blindsided by my diagnosis. The severity of the cancer meant my bladder had to be removed, and then I was dosed with toxic chemo for four months. Yet I am one of the lucky ones: I am still alive and now healthy.

All the attendees that evening had been moved by Darrell's words, so when I asked for a couple of minutes to gather my thoughts before beginning the auction, they were gracious. At night's end, the generous guests had raised over $200,000, with a replica of Terry's shoes bringing the biggest bidding frenzy. When we presented the cheque to Darrell, he thanked the crowd and shared Terry's famous quote: "I want to set an example that will never be forgotten." For a second time that evening, there wasn't a dry eye in the house.

I learned so much about Terry that night. Darrell shared how determined Terry was to get approval to attempt the cross-Canada run. His mom initially disapproved, as did his best friend, his doctor, and the Canadian Cancer Society. They called him a dreamer. His response was, "I just wish people would realize that anything is possible if you try, dreams are made possible if you try."

Learning about Terry's incredible dedication motivated me to do more. A few months after the fundraiser in Banff, the Fox family located the original van that was used during the Marathon of Hope. Darrell asked if I had any ideas of what to do with this treasure. "A cross-country tour, from St. John's to Victoria with many stops, so the entire country can see the van first-hand and meet a family member," I suggested. "And we could call it the Tour of Hope!"

The family was thrilled with the concept and I started planning the tour. The vehicle was refurbished, and in the summer of 2008, it made its way slowly across this great country, accompanied by rotating Fox family members. During our stop in Ottawa, I witnessed a young lady come up to Terry's mother, Betty, and ask if she could give her a hug. "Of course you can," Betty replied. After the lengthy embrace, the young lady rolled up her pant leg and revealed her Terry Fox tattoo. In Toronto, the family drove the van onto the Blue Jays' baseball field and received a standing ovation; the players even wore their retro 1980 uniforms as a tribute to Terry. Thanks to all the volunteers who eagerly assisted, the Tour of Hope raised over $500,000 for the Terry Fox Foundation.

A few years later, I was treated to a heartwarming workshop performance of a Terry Fox musical by the talented John Connolly of Sheridan College. Curious about future plans for the show, I reached out and learned of John's dream for as many Canadians as possible to see it. I teamed up with him to help, and thanks to the great people at Drayton Entertainment, over 30,000 theatre-goers have now seen *Marathon of Hope: The Musical*. We were able to raise over $100,000 in donations during the musical's run, and we plan to tour it across Canada.

It has been an honour to be a part of keeping Terry's dream alive, and I am privileged to continue learning about Terry along the way. The more stories I hear, the more impressed I am with this remarkably humble, determined, and courageous hero. I've also come to realize that we need to recognize the real heroes who have kept his dream alive.

"I've said to people before that I'm going to do my very best to make it, I'm not going to give up. But I might not make it . . . if I don't, the Marathon of Hope better continue." Mother Betty, father Rolly, and siblings Fred, Darrell, and Judy took Terry's wishes to heart and have dedicated their lives to his dream while respecting his values. Much has been written about Terry's courage, perseverance, and dedication—the same can be said for the entire Fox family. For the last forty years, they have travelled across this great country visiting schools, community gatherings, and fundraisers to share the incredible journey Terry endured for the benefit of others. Over one million children have listened to a Fox family member share Terry's values of integrity, caring, and inclusiveness. In true Terry Fox style, they want to ensure that every dollar donated goes to cancer research, so whenever possible they take public transit and bunk up at a friend's house when touring. While it was Terry's journey that left us in awe, I have also been inspired by the lifetimes of effort from Terry's adoring family.

Terry, you would be very proud of your family; they were listening when you said, "Never give up on your dreams." They have never faltered in keeping your legacy alive. Your family and Canadians across the country will never give up on your dream. It is the least we can do.

Fox family photo from the first years the family lived in British Columbia.

As was everything Terry did, his stamina was truly unmatchable. He ran through pain, exhaustion, and against the wind for a dream, for a better future, for us.

Malindi Elmore

MALINDI ELMORE IS a track-and-field athlete and coach. A
2004 Olympian, in January 2020 Malindi set the Canadian
women's record for the marathon with a time of 2:24:50. Prior
to her professional athletic career, she was a five-time All-
American athlete at Stanford University and held the school's
records in the 800-metre and 1,500-metre events. Malindi
lives in Kelowna, B.C., with her husband and two kids.

Even now when I think of the Marathon of Hope, I cannot
believe that Terry was able to run a marathon every single
day. I spent four months training for the marathon I ran in
January 2020 and then took a month of recovery afterward.
The fact that Terry ran the equivalent of a forty-two-kilometre
marathon day after day—for 143 days—is really mind-boggling.
Nobody in the world runs 300 kilometres in a week, not even
elite runners who put in the highest mileage. What Terry did
is unheard of. His body must have taken such a physical toll
and been so fatigued, and yet he found the motivation to get
up every day and start all over again. He showed incredible
stamina running through pain, exhaustion, and harsh condi-
tions. Terry was truly spectacular.

I like to imagine what he might have been thinking while he ran. A lot of times, I have my best ideas while I'm running because I find it relaxing. My brain has the space to actually be free, so I let my thoughts wander. Quite often, though, I'm focused on my goals and the task at hand because I want to perform well. I imagine a lot of Terry's thoughts were focused on what his purpose was, what he had to accomplish each day to achieve his goal. Many of his best ideas about what needed to happen to make the Marathon of Hope a success probably came to him while he was running. And I think that's one of the great things about the sport: when you have real purpose, it's motivating—and it also consumes a lot of your headspace while you're putting one foot in front of the other.

I imagine Terry also had a lot of profound moments, reflecting on his purpose in life. There are moments that you have in the middle of a run when things become clear. If Terry thought about his own mortality, which is a scary thought for anyone, I hope he found a certain amount of peace over the course of his runs. He couldn't have known then how much of a legacy he would leave behind, but he believed in what he was doing. Terry's deep, burning desire to make it a successful campaign kept him going when I'm sure it felt like his legs could not.

Aside from the sheer mileage he covered, there are many details that make his run even more challenging than it would be now. For one, clothing wasn't as sophisticated in 1980. He was running in a cotton T-shirt and a pair of cotton shorts, which wouldn't have wicked sweat away from the body. That alone would be uncomfortable and could have caused chafing or blisters. Nutrition for runners has become a lot more scientific since then, too. Thanks to advances in sport science, we can now pinpoint how many grams of carbohydrates a runner needs to consume every hour they are training or competing, based on details like their weight, sweat rate, the temperature and humidity they are running in, and even the strength of the wind. Terry tackled his cross-country journey with a brother, a friend, a camper van, and some bare essentials. There were likely many hit or miss days and figuring things out on the fly.

Whether you're a runner or not, Terry is a unifying hero for all Canadians. He was so brave in the face of adversity. From coast to coast, he rallied people to support cancer research. I know he had a hard time getting people to pay attention and donate at the beginning of his run, and that must have been frustrating. Incredibly, he persevered and managed to put cancer in the forefront of Canadians' minds at a time when there was no social media. And he held himself so well when the mainstream media began to follow his run. That was impressive because he was such a young man, and most people are still trying to figure out who they are at that age.

To me, Terry is the most essential Canadian in our history because he bound us all together. With every step that he took, he united a nation and compelled people to take up the fight against cancer. Running has never been more beautiful.

Through my friendship with Terry, and from watching everything he did, from fundraising to training, he taught me how to embrace the values he stuck to so strongly.

Jay Triano

JAY TRIANO IS assistant coach of the Charlotte Hornets basketball team. He became the first Canadian-born head coach in
the NBA when he served in that role for the Toronto Raptors,
later becoming interim head coach of the Phoenix Suns. Prior
to coaching in the NBA, Jay played basketball for Simon Fraser
University, competed in two Olympic Games as a player, and
served as head coach of the Canadian men's team for the 2000
Summer Olympics in Sydney.

Terry was one of the first people I met at Simon Fraser
University (SFU). I'd been recruited to play basketball and
left my parents' home in Niagara Falls, arriving in B.C. the last
week of August 1977. I got there early, thinking I'd have a week
to prepare for school, but I didn't anticipate that I would be so
lonely. There were no other students there yet. I remember
going to the coach's office—and Terry was sitting there. I'd
heard about him and I didn't know what to say. I was going in
to complain about being homesick, and here was this guy who
was very similar to me, both in age and the love we shared for
basketball, and he'd lost his leg to cancer. We chatted briefly,
and after he left, I knew better than to complain. Instead, I
told coach Stan Stewardson that I felt bad because I hadn't

known what to say to Terry. He said, "Don't worry. He's going to be our manager, so he'll be around all the time."

Terry and I started to build a friendship. As the manager of our junior varsity team, he did everything. He taped ankles. He learned how to become a trainer. He took care of all the little things that needed to be done around the gym. We spent a lot of time together. Eventually, we started talking about our goals. He always said, "I'm going to run across Canada. I can't believe what I saw in the cancer ward and how many children are suffering. I have to do something to help." His goal was to raise money for cancer research. We talked a lot about his dream, and I shared my hopes of becoming an Olympic athlete.

He was so determined. Whenever I went to train at the university, I'd jump on a bus to take me up Burnaby Mountain. I'd look out the window of the bus, which was grinding just to make the climb, and there was Terry wheeling his wheelchair up the mountain. I thought, "This guy is more dedicated to his dream than I am!" I'd be in the gym and Terry would show up, dripping with sweat and ready to start his workout—after going two miles up a mountain. He'd say, "I can't stop when I'm going up because I'd start rolling backward. I've just got to keep going." Seeing his effort was extremely motivating: it made me want to work harder, too.

During that time, Terry started holding weekly fundraising dances in SFU's east gymnasium. He was trying to raise the money he would need to run across the country. No one other than our basketball team showed up to the first dance, and I remember feeling bad. But Terry was as persistent with those dances as he was with everything else. By the end of the semester, his dances were known as the fun thing to do and the gym was packed. I don't remember if he managed to raise much money, but I know we all had fun.

Terry had a dream, and watching him tackle the steps to accomplish it was inspiring. When he started his run, I followed his progress across the country. I'd been training with the Canadian men's national team to prepare for the 1980 Olympic qualifying games when I heard that Terry wanted to visit me in Niagara Falls. Shortly after he arrived in Toronto, Terry took half of a day off from the Marathon of Hope and flew to meet me in my hometown. I'd like to tell you that our visit was deep and meaningful, but it was more along the lines of "How are you doing?" He wanted to know about my experiences with the national team and I wanted to hear how the run was going. He talked about how hard it was to run a marathon every single day, how his body was taking a beating. It was general stuff, but we were just two friends catching up.

The last times I saw Terry were back at SFU, after he'd travelled home to receive treatment for his cancer. He would come out to watch our games and we'd talk in the stands afterward. One time, he asked me to autograph something, and I said, "Are you kidding me? You're my idol. You're the guy who's raised all this awareness and money for cancer research. You've invigorated all of Canada. *I'm* the one who needs the autograph." Of course, Terry was so modest. What he did was never about him: it was about the people he was trying to help. He instilled in me the desire to make someone else's day better—and that's one of the reasons I'm coaching now. Terry showed me how important it is to help other people achieve their goals and dreams.

I haven't been back to SFU in a long time, but for me, the school will forever be synonymous with Terry Fox. I met him there, we worked hard there, and we became friends there. There isn't a time I've driven up that long mountain road and not thought of him wheeling up it. When I envision Terry these days, I like to picture him running around the school's track. He was always at home when he was running.

Terry's SFU student ID card, 1978.

We could only hope to amplify Terry's message with our broadcast and telethon—nothing could have spoken as loud as his actions already had.

Lloyd Robertson

LLOYD ROBERTSON IS one of Canada's most well-known and respected journalists. He anchored *CTV National News* for thirty-five years, a position that gave him what he has described as a front-row seat to history.

On Monday, September 1, 1980, outside of Thunder Bay, Ontario, Terry made his tearful announcement that he was stopping his run because his cancer had returned. Right away, CTV's management group, keenly aware of how Canadians had taken Terry into their hearts, said they wanted to do something to support his mission. It was almost immediately decided that we'd mount a telethon to add as much as we could to Terry's war chest against cancer.

As I sat down in the studio chair that Sunday evening, I struggled with how to open the telethon. There had been little time to prepare, the set had been hastily thrown together, and there was no script. I desperately wanted to hit the right tone: one that would honour and continue Terry's dream—the dream that he had instilled in all of us. Our telethon could never be as inspiring as Terry's run, but we hoped to continue fundraising in the way we knew best. I had never tackled anything like this before, and five minutes before the start of the show, I was still trying to work it out in my head.

At that moment, CTV executive Arthur Weinthal, a real pro when it came to broadcasting, walked up to me and said, "Remember, Lloyd, this is a celebration of courage." That's what we ultimately titled the broadcast. It was exactly the right note, and it was how I opened the Marathon of Hope telethon: "Tonight is a celebration of courage." Every single minute from almost every part of Canada, 750 people were on the phone calling in pledges, and every single minute, the total jumped by $25,000. The event raised $10.5 million in just five hours. Terry was watching the broadcast from his hospital room, and we were told he was completely moved to tears.

Many have tried to explain the Terry phenomenon. Media personality Sook-Yin Lee, in her presentation of Terry's story for CBC's *The Greatest Canadian* series, described his attributes as "the perfect mix of compassion, commitment, and perseverance." At the 2010 Winter Paralympics in Vancouver, where Betty and Rolly Fox were torchbearers, athletes were presented with a medal in Terry's name that cited "determination and humility in the face of adversity."

My own take on Terry and his profound impact is this: he was a regular kid, one who everyone knows, our next-door neighbour or the kid down the block. No one would have begrudged him for being upset or angry that he had been hit by cancer at such a young age. What makes Terry exceptional is that he didn't let resentment or self-pity in. He set out to do something about his plight and to make a difference.

There was nothing posed or phony about him. He was all gritty reality as he headed out across the country. He struck a chord, reminding us of the toughness of so many Canadians, a product of our rugged landscape and challenging climate. We are hearty people at the core and Terry reminds us of that.

As a news story, Terry's journey affected me as few others have, in the sense that it was so personal and emotional. We all had family members, neighbours, and friends touched by cancer in some way. Everybody felt it. Everybody felt as if this young man was speaking directly to them. I met Terry when he was passing through Toronto during the Marathon of Hope and did a brief interview with him. I was struck by his calm yet determined demeanour. Here was just an average kid on this marathon mission because he believed so deeply in finding a cure for cancer. He was saying to his generation, "This is something we have to fight." Terry was one of the first to instill in us the belief that cancer can be beaten.

His message is one that has resonated deeply within my own family. Ten years after Terry passed, our daughter Susan was diagnosed with cancer in her late twenties. Her tumour was soon removed, and I took a cue from Terry during the difficult moments, telling her, "Remember, you're tough. You're resilient. You'll come through this." Susan was ultimately cleared of cancer, and I was proud to serve for a full year as chairman of the Terry Fox Run.

Terry did not survive his cancer, but he raised the profile of the fight against the disease with millions of dollars raised in his name all over the world. Progress has been made but the fight is far from over: there are still cancers that are rigidly resistant to treatment. Terry showed us how one person can make a difference when we care enough to pour heart and soul into a cause. That's why Terry's story has been, and forever will be, a legend that's worth keeping alive.

Terry was, and still is, the epitome of perseverance, endurance, and toughness.

Mary Hardisty

MARY HARDISTY JOINED the Ontario Provincial Police (OPP) in 1979. Now retired, Mary lives in Stayner, Ontario, with her husband, Steve, who is also a retired OPP officer.

I was in awe of Terry Fox before I even met him. I remember watching him on the news and seeing him dip his leg into the Atlantic Ocean at the start of the Marathon of Hope. I continued to follow his story and read about his near misses on the highway while making his way across the Maritimes and Quebec. As a police officer, those near misses distressed me very much, and I was relieved to learn that the Ontario Provincial Police had committed to providing him with a police escort while he made his way through our province.

At that time, I had only been an officer for ten months and was about to return to the Ontario Police College to complete my basic training. Upon arriving at work for a midnight shift, I found a note from my shift supervisor instructing me to meet Terry Fox at the Lake Joseph Motel at five a.m. I was thrilled to receive the honour of escorting Terry.

At the motel, I introduced myself to Terry, and we shook hands. I found him to be quite shy, but it was pretty early in the morning and he had a huge day in front of him. This was in July 1980, right around Terry's twenty-second birthday; for a few short weeks, Terry and I were the same age. I really admired him for making such a positive impact out of negative circumstances.

A member of Terry's team briefed me on the procedure: the van drove in front of Terry and I would be behind him with the roof lights going; Terry took a break in the van every few miles. I drove behind Terry for about six hours, and I was amazed to think that in a relativity short period of time, he had made it to Ontario from Newfoundland. People driving in the opposite lane honked their support to Terry, and he waved in acknowledgment.

One stretch of Highway 69 is quite steep, and I remember thinking to myself, "Terry, just get in the cruiser for this part of the highway. No one would know!" Of course, that was never an option for him. Dawn was just breaking as Terry ran up that hill. Twenty years later—almost to the day—I returned to that very spot, when I brought my young son to Camp Oochigeas, a camp for kids with cancer. Every time I see that hill, I relive that early morning, watching Terry persevere up that steep incline.

Around ten-thirty or so, another officer came to relieve me. I went over to the van to say goodbye just as Terry was finishing up a rest. I wished him great success in his marathon, and he thanked me for escorting him and for the good wishes. We shook hands again and he went on his way, continuing his run.

As I was driving out of town that afternoon, I spotted Terry farther down the highway. The road was absolutely packed with people and cars. I managed to find a spot to park and quickly snapped a photo. When I processed the film weeks later, I was amazed to find that I had gotten a shot of just Terry with the Welcome to Parry Sound sign in the background.

I was back at police college when the announcement came that Terry had been forced to stop his run. I was upset for Terry that he could not complete his Marathon of Hope and was devastated to learn that his cancer had returned. I took some solace in the deserved attention that his Marathon of Hope received and that the fundraising and awareness of cancer research didn't die with Terry.

Nine years after I escorted Terry, my son, Raymond, was born with a rare blood disorder. By the time he was four, it had developed into leukemia. We spent much of the next eighteen years at SickKids while he battled this disease, received a bone marrow transplant, and suffered complications that left him physically disabled. I can't really point to a specific time when Raymond became aware of Terry Fox, but his story has always been a huge part of our lives. That photo I took of Terry has been displayed in our home since 1980, and I put the photo on a T-shirt for Raymond to wear in Terry Fox Runs when he was in school.

Much like Terry, Raymond has taken fundraising to heart. Influenced by the years he spent at SickKids and by his job at our local Dairy Queen, Raymond focuses his fundraising efforts in support of Children's Miracle Network, which raises money for local children's hospitals. He takes it very seriously and increases his goal every year, not only because of his extensive stays at SickKids and cancer battle but also because of what Terry Fox did and what his legacy continues to inspire. I couldn't have imagined the influence Terry would come to have on my family during that pre-dawn morning in 1980. Terry's spirit has remained with us ever since. I imagine Terry would be blown away by the huge impact he has made not only on Canada but on the world.

I vividly remember something a colleague told me years ago, after I had mentioned that I met Terry Fox and shook his hand twice. He said, "Wow, you shook the hand that shook the world." I couldn't agree more.

Water Terry collected from the Atlantic, before commencing his marathon.
He intended to pour this water into the Pacific, after completing his run across
the country.

The truest of champions, who brought Canada together onto one team.

Kim Gaucher

KIM GAUCHER IS one of Canada's most accomplished professional women's basketball players. She represented Canada in the 2012 and 2016 Olympic Games, captained Canada in four FIBA Basketball World Cups, and helped Team Canada win gold at the Toronto 2015 Pan-Am Games. Kim is one of only two players in U.S. college history to win their conference player of the year award all four years, was a first-round pick in the 2006 WNBA draft, and is one of few Canadians to have played in the WNBA finals.

Growing up in B.C.'s lower mainland, it is almost impossible to not know the name Terry Fox. His name adorns the streets we live on, the schools we attend, and the parks, courts, and fields we play on. His fundraisers run through our streets and statues of him are all around. He was one of us.

But to know the name and to know the story are two different things. Being born in 1984, I did not have a direct connection to the Marathon of Hope, but my parents always counted him as one of the greatest athletes and people this country has ever produced. Somewhere around the fifth grade, I was given Leslie Scrivener's book *Terry Fox: His Story*. Learning about his work ethic, perseverance, and stubbornness changed me, and I often reread that book and give to friends from around the world.

Through sports, I have been able to make a living and travel the world, and I've learned a lot of life's lessons. However, never in my career have I been confused with being the biggest, fastest, or strongest. At a young age, I learned from people like Terry Fox that you don't always have to be the most talented at something. If you have the drive and the dedication, incredible things can happen. Looking back on my basketball career, incredible is the best way to describe it. I didn't start out with exceptional talent: I worked really hard in order to get better.

I learned about Terry's determination not just from the book but from Mike McNeill, who was an assistant coach for the women's national basketball team for many years. Mike played basketball at Simon Fraser University and eventually went on to coach there. He said that when Terry made the junior varsity team, there were more talented players who didn't make the cut. As Mike once told the Terry Fox Foundation, "Terry just out-gutted them. People tend to look in awe at players who have a lot of natural ability, but respect from other athletes goes to the guy who works really hard." I have an unbelievable amount of respect for the work Terry put into his pursuits, be they on the court or the side of the highway.

The resiliency Terry showed astonishes me to this day— the way he handled his cancer diagnosis and the news that he would lose his leg, and how he transitioned his life and

purpose and energy into something else, something that
became so huge that it's almost unimaginable.

I am a huge believer in the idea that it is the little things
in life, when all added up, that make the big things possible.
I'm sure Terry thought of the Marathon of Hope in the same
way, because the big picture would be so hard to tackle. But
he broke it down into segments, aiming for the next rest stop,
the next marker. And he started running every morning at the
exact spot he had finished the night before. That attention to
detail and level of personal accountability speaks to the high-
level athlete he was. All good athletes know that if you cut
corners, you might make some ground in the short term but
you only hurt yourself in the long term.

He also just seemed like someone who liked being part of a
team. Even after Terry lost his leg to cancer, he stayed on the
SFU basketball team as a manager. Locker rooms are incredible places of friendship and togetherness but also a thera-
peutic place and a way to stay sane. My parents thought I was
way too shy as a kid and that a team sport would be good for
me—they were right!

When I finally get some time to go home and visit my family in Mission, B.C., I still work out at one of the same gyms
I've spent countless weekends at in Port Coquitlam. It never
matters how tired, jet-lagged, sore, or uninspired I am that
day because when I approach Terry Fox Secondary and see his
statue, it's impossible to not feel a little pep in my step and
to stand a little taller. It has always been one of my favourite
gyms to play in.

Knowing his story, reflecting on his experiences, imagining what his feelings and emotions must have been, I understand why my parents put him up there with the finest our country has to offer. Making the best of a terrible situation, inspiring others to do more, paying attention to detail, plus a relentless work ethic are what every parent wants their kids to learn. Terry Fox: the truest of champions and the greatest of Canadians.

Terry loved team sports—here, he is around 8 or 9 years old, with a baseball trophy.

Fred Fox and I continuing the good fight for Terry.

Bret Hart

BRET "HITMAN" HART is recognized around the world as one of pro wrestling's all-time greats. He has been inducted into both the WWE Hall of Fame and the George Tragos/Lou Thesz Professional Wrestling Hall of Fame.

People throw around the word "hero" too easily these days. But when I think about Terry, I'm reminded *that's* a real hero. I remember the summer he did his run. I was young, living the life of a twenty-three-year-old wrestler, and I had a lot on my mind. But what Terry Fox did grabbed me. My dad had a couple of vans he drove the wrestlers around in and I was always in one of those vans, driving up and down the TransCanada in Alberta and Saskatchewan, thinking, "Terry's coming. Any week now, we're going to see him." I was tracking his progress, and we knew we'd eventually see him coming down the road. You know, as all-consuming as my life as a wrestler was back in those days, Terry's commitment was a powerful message that broke through to me, and he connected with people my age. To devote himself as tirelessly as he did at the end of the road was amazing, and to raise the awareness he did, at a time when there was no Internet or social media, was incredible. When the news came that he had to pull out of the run, it was heartbreaking.

As a professional wrestler, you're called upon to support
different charities all the time. The Terry Fox Foundation
is one of the few that I would do anything for. I've seen how
committed the people are and I know they do a lot of good
things. For my part, I was happy to be the spokesperson for
Calgary's Terry Fox Run a few years back. It meant a lot to me.
My brother, Smith, had just died from prostate cancer. He
had never been screened for prostate cancer, and by the time
he started to have issues and they found out it was cancer, it
was too late. I've had prostate cancer, too, but thankfully my
doctors had been monitoring me since I was forty and saw
the rise in my PSA level, the marker indicating cancerous
cells. When they eventually said to me, "You have cancer,"
it was like my heart fell out of my chest. It was very sobering and very scary. I had surgery and have had a clean bill of
health since. So, I was excited to get involved with the Terry
Fox Fun and to support the cause; the money that's being
raised is critical. Amazing things are happening in cancer
research every day. They're getting closer to a cure. And the
Terry Fox Run is raising money to see it through.

The run has proved to be good for family bonding, too. I'm
constantly trying to drum up unity and support because there's
been a lot of dissension in my family. After my brother Owen
died during a wrestling stunt in 1999, it was like family members took different sides. Some people just don't get along
with each other anymore, and those dynamics have lingered
for a long time. But the Terry Fox Run is bringing us closer
together. Even though you might not want to make peace

with your brother, you can do it for Terry's sake. I lay on the guilt trip sometimes and say, "Don't do it for you. Don't do it for the family. Do it for Terry." Now we have a bigger group of Harts coming out every year, even the holdouts who have been mad about stuff for a long time. It's like everyone's kind of put down their arms. People who weren't getting along are getting along, and it's thanks to Terry.

These days, I never go very far when we do the run. I had a stroke in 2002 and my left side didn't come back very well, so I don't have the same ability as I used to. At the same time, I don't believe that the purpose of the run is the distance you go—it's about the message. The run, for me, is about the cause and the legend, Terry Fox. To deal with his circumstances the way that he did and to raise all that money . . . it's an amazing story. I think it's one of the best. He did such a great job of fulfilling what seemed like a lofty dream and I'm sure his family, along with everybody who ever knew him, is proud of what he pulled off. He's an iconic symbol, a Canadian hero. I didn't know him, but Terry Fox sure makes *me* proud.

The man whose unconquerable spirit and feats rallied the country, with his mother, Betty.

Steve Nash

DURING HIS EIGHTEEN seasons in the National Basketball Association (NBA), Steve Nash, O.C., was named the NBA's Most Valuable Player twice, selected as an NBA All-Star eight times, and was inducted into the Naismith Memorial Basketball Hall of Fame in 2018. In 2010, Steve co-directed the award-winning ESPN short documentary on Terry, *Into the Wind*. Raised in Victoria, B.C., Steve currently lives with his family in California and serves as president of the Steve Nash Foundation, an organization dedicated to fostering health in kids, and as a team owner, television sports analyst, and NBA player development coach.

Terry's story speaks for itself, in a lot of ways—the invincibility, the humanity, the hope. As a six-year-old kid in British Columbia, his attempt to run across Canada took me in completely. On a little TV in my Oak Bay home that we had to turn on with tweezers, I watched every morning, as soon as I woke up, to see where Terry was. All of my friends did. Our hometown of Victoria was just before his finish line, and we felt like part of the pull, leading him west.

When Terry ran, somehow I didn't see the struggle. I saw the strength. When I catch that footage now, I still do. It was impossible to watch him and not see how different his running looked compared to mine, yet his movement was so rhythmic, so solid, that it was the runner that came through. His mind-set was all over his face, in the way he held himself, in his silent steadiness. That made such an impression on me—it was maybe my first real exposure to the grit of resilience. I remember hearing that his prosthetic leg was so painful that he bled from it, and maybe we even saw that in the news coverage. But with Terry, everything was aligned and working with purpose. He passed on that determination to so many of us that I think it's more than a piece of our cultural fabric—generations of Canadians impacted by this "regular" guy's dedication to change.

There were things I didn't think about back then—I don't think I ever wondered whether Terry thought his cancer was terminal. I believed that he was going to follow what was later described to me as a "meticulous plan" to make it, and that we'd all be there to see him dip his foot in the Pacific. When he suspended the run, I thought it was only temporary, a pause to recover. Because what could interrupt, let alone defeat, that kind of indomitable spirit? That spirit was contagious. When we interviewed Terry's mother, Betty, about the day Terry called her to say his cancer had returned, had spread, I felt even some measure of surprise from her, all those years later. So while Terry felt his vulnerability as a kindred connection to all those he sought to help—"I'm just like everybody else"—to me, and

maybe many of those watching his run, Terry's strength somehow ruled out the possibility of his own mortality.

We probably do that too much—lionize people to such an
extent that we don't allow their own humanity to breathe.
As an adult, I had the incredible opportunity to get to know
so much more of the story and the person through visits
with Terry's family, friends, and some of the people who had
watched his marathon as I had. Listening to Betty sum up her
son's determination, even obstinance, in the face of cautious
doubters with a terse "tough titty"; his friend Jay laugh, remem-
bering Terry's conviction, and Doug talk about the day-to-day
struggles of a friendship lived in the closest of quarters as they
drove thousands of miles together; hearing his brother Darrell
list off the medical ramifications of Terry's illness, from the
toll chemo took on his heart to the effect of running in the heat
of summer; and reading in Terry's journals his own self-talk
on the doubts that plague so many athletes—I found a deeper
connection to the man behind the legendary status that he
had held for me throughout my life.

Now I think Terry probably was aware that cancer would
end his road, which makes it all the more inspiring: in the
face of that crushing weight, he hustled for change, to help
others. No sitting, no moping, just drive and hustle for
change that wouldn't come in time to save him. That sense of
constantly impelling forward has held such force in my life,
as I'm sure it has for millions of others.

The autumn after Terry died, the first Terry Fox Run was
held in Victoria, and all of my friends were there. Every year

growing up, it was simply what we did, and our thoughts
of Terry pushed us to run without stopping. My friends at
home still do the run, now with their kids, all of us, maybe,
acknowledging not only Terry's heroism but the human vul-
nerabilities that tie us all together.

Terry was my hero as a kid. Back then, I asked him so many
questions, and throughout my life, he's given me so many
answers. He inspired me to go for it. To believe in myself.
To get to work. Twenty-five years after Terry had rallied the
country with his improbable run into Toronto, I stood in front
of thousands in Nathan Phillips Square, too. Although I'm
sure no one else present thought about it, the moment wasn't
lost on this undersized, basketball-playing kid from B.C.
who had learned from the best how to be hopeful, in the face
of all the world's frailties, inspired, and determined to keep
pushing for change.

Port Coquitlam High School, Grade 11 basketball team. Terry is #4, his favourite number.

The powerful end to our cross-country relay run; having Terry's statue as our finish line.

Akshay Grover

AKSHAY GROVER IS an avid runner. In 2018, he organized a
relay run from Montreal to Vancouver to raise money for the
Terry Fox Foundation. Akshay graduated from Concordia
University in May 2020 with a bachelor degree in communica-
tions and currently lives in Montreal, Quebec.

I've always loved long-distance running. At my high school,
each student had to come up with a personal project to meet
the graduation requirements; I realized that, like Terry, I
could use my running to accomplish something. I decided to
run from Montreal to Toronto, with my mom following me
in her car, to raise money to fight childhood cancer. I spent
fourteen days on the road and it was hard, but I managed to
raise $14,000. After that, friends from my track team wanted
to get involved, too, so we formed the Montreal Runners
team. We planned a cross-border run to support the Terry Fox
Foundation: if you're going to run for a cause in Canada, no
one deserves it more than Terry. In 2016, four of us ran from
Montreal to Washington, D.C., hoping to raise awareness and
to encourage other young people to get involved. We covered
close to 1,000 kilometres in ten days. At the end, we knew we

had more left to give—and that's when we came up with the idea to run from Montreal to Vancouver.

In June 2018, after I had finished my first year at Concordia University, six of us set out on the run. Keiston Herchel, Muhan Patel, twin brothers Marc-André and Matthieu Blouin, Declan McCool, and I covered 180 kilometres every day, with each person running thirty kilometres. We alternated runners every five kilometres so we had a chance to rest in our vans in between, and we followed the route Terry took from Montreal to Thunder Bay. For the forty-two kilometres leading to Thunder Bay, we ran a silent marathon in honour of Terry. Our run became real when we reached his monument there. We were roughly the same age that Terry had been when he ran the Marathon of Hope, and we realized how courageous he was to run alone. We had each other to lean on, which made the early mornings and long days easier.

Every day, we woke up at five in the morning, had a short warm-up, and ate a massive breakfast. Aside from snacking on granola bars in the vans, we didn't eat again until we'd finished running for the day. Nighttime is when we really witnessed Canadians' hospitality. Months before our run began, Keiston had sent emails to campgrounds, motels, and Airbnbs to tell them about our trip and let them know we were on our way. Almost everyone has been affected by cancer in some way, so people were incredibly supportive of what we were doing. Most offered us free or heavily discounted accommodations, and many went the extra mile by making us food. We saw first-hand how much love people still have for Terry. Once, while I was running on the side of the highway in Saskatchewan, a woman stopped to ask if I needed help. I said, "No, thanks. My friends and I are running from Montreal to Vancouver to raise money for cancer research." She said, "Oh really? Here's ten dollars." She handed over a bill, and I said, "Thanks so much. We're doing this for the Terry Fox Foundation." She took out another bill and said, "Here's another ten for Terry."

Running is such a mental sport. When you're hurting, you make little goals for yourself in order to keep going, knowing you still have many kilometres to go. I can't imagine how Terry did what he did, day after day, month after month. The example of his perseverance helped us through the most gruelling parts of our run, especially as we ran through the Rockies. It wasn't easy and a couple of us were injured by the time we closed in on Vancouver, but the end was in sight.

I'll never forget the last day. We had planned to run together for the first time since leaving Montreal and to finish at Terry's statue at Simon Fraser University. The emotion of it all set in as we ran up the huge hill leading to the school. When we finally made it to Terry's statue, we huddled up, linked arms, and held onto each other. It was our quiet moment to reflect on what we had just done—and to salute our hero.

Growing up, I always felt that Terry was a larger-than-life figure. Eventually I realized the most beautiful thing about Terry Fox is that he was an ordinary Canadian who wanted to make a difference. His monument in Thunder Bay has an inscription that reads, "To every Canadian, he left us a

challenge—a challenge each of us will meet in our own way."
I think about that a lot. On my last big run, my friends and I
covered 4,632 kilometres over thirty days and raised about
$36,000, an effort I hope would have made Terry happy.
Today, we like speaking at schools to share his message and
encourage kids to get involved, to meet his challenge in their
own way. We let them know Terry was just like them: young,
capable, and ready to change the world.

It was not the norm for people to run with Terry. When they did, they would run behind him.

For a young man such as Terry, with his steadfast dedication to achieve a better future, I wish that I could have contributed much more than just an RV.

Jim Pattison

JIM PATTISON IS CEO, chairman, and owner of the Jim Pattison Group, one of Canada's largest privately held companies. A renowned businessperson and philanthropist, he has been appointed to the Order of Canada and the Order of British Columbia, and has been inducted into Canada's Walk of Fame, among other honours. In 1980, Jim donated an RV for Terry Fox to use on the latter part of his Marathon of Hope.

Over the years, my company has been asked to donate to many charities. I've always asked myself one question in order to decide whether or not to support an organization: will its work make a difference? The minute we heard about Terry Fox, we knew he would make a difference in this world—and we wanted to help him. We donated an RV for Terry to use during his Marathon of Hope. Watching him set out on his journey was really something. Terry had big dreams. As a company that has always dreamed big, we respected his mission. He was determined to have an impact, to give all of himself no matter how difficult the journey was.

My father was the first person to teach me the importance of giving back. We didn't have a lot of money when I was growing up, and I remember getting my weekly fifty-cent allowance.

We'd go to church and my dad would say, "Now, Jimmy, make sure you put five cents in the collection plate." I did, and the lesson I learned from an early age was that it's important to give, even when you have little yourself.

That guiding belief is one I share with the Terry Fox Foundation. Whether it's a child donating one dollar or an organization giving millions, the foundation celebrates every gift equally. The Jim Pattison Group admires that about the foundation, not to mention how dedicated the whole Fox family is to upholding Terry's legacy in such a personal and humble way. It's remarkable, and it's why we've been happy to help the cause from time to time since Terry's run. (When the family asked if I'd volunteer to shave heads at a fundraiser in 2007, I didn't realize I'd be shaving Terry's father's head, among others!)

When we as Canadians look back at Terry's run and everything that the foundation has accomplished since, we are in awe. He achieved even more than he set out to do. Terry found it within himself to give, to make a profound difference that continues to reverberate and inspire people today. May we all work together to carry his big dream and vision into tomorrow.

Betty Fox, like any Mom, loved family photos.

A beautiful, necessary reminder of the challenge Terry dedicated himself to, one that is called to mind as we travel on roads that carry his name.

Silken Laumann

SILKEN LAUMANN IS a Canadian Olympic medallist and World Champion in rowing. She is also an author, activist, motivational speaker, and creator of *Unsinkable*, a web-based story-sharing project that connects Canadians to each other and to stories that unite, inspire, motivate, inform, and support whole health and well-being.

I have yet to meet a Canadian who doesn't recognize the name Terry Fox. He is literally a Canadian icon: he is commemorated on a coin, on our stamps, and in various museums across the country. There are schools and a mountain named after him, and there is a ten-foot statue of Terry right here in my hometown of Victoria, B.C. The statue stands at Mile Zero, which, depending on the coast you relate to, marks either the beginning or end of our country. It is the mile marker that Terry set his sights on when he began his cross-Canada run to raise money for cancer research all those years ago.

All the physical commemorations of Terry are important to keep his legacy alive, but to me, corny as it may sound, Terry lives on in people's hearts in a much bigger way. His story and his courage got under our collective skin; it permeated our bodies, it stirred our souls, and, as a result, there is a little bit of his spirit in everyone who pursues excellence, social change, or acts of bravery and service.

The only time I saw Terry Fox was through a crowd of 10,000 in Nathan Phillips Square. I was a wide-eyed young athlete pursuing her dream of being an Olympic runner, and I had heard about a guy planning to run across Canada one marathon per day *after he had lost a leg to cancer* to fundraise for cancer research. I had to see him in person to believe that he was real. I didn't get particularly close to the stage where Terry stood, but his energy and the energy of what he was doing changed me that day, as it did millions of Canadians.

It is of extra-special significance to me now, so many years after I was in that crowd, that Terry and I literally connect: in Mississauga, Ontario, where Terry Fox Way becomes Silken Laumann Way. That one of my life's greatest honours ties me to one of my lifelong heroes is something I will always deeply treasure.

I was lucky to have been gifted with the size and strength to propel a rowing shell quickly through the water and to possess a true passion for the beautiful sport of rowing. My path to Olympic success and World Championship wins was not a linear one. Self-doubt was my greatest adversary, something I came to identify and conquer later in my career. What Canadians recognize me for most is overcoming a near career-ending accident ten weeks before the 1992 Olympic Games in Barcelona, Spain. I was the defending World Champion and World Cup Champion when I had an accident in Essen, Germany, that threatened to end my rowing career. While on the water, a men's pair collided into my wooden single scull, shattering the splashboard and driving 200 splinters of wood into my lower right leg. The doctors confirmed the devastating damage: shredded muscle, broken bone, nerve damage, and massive skin damage. I was told the Olympics were over for me. But I had a dream, I had a goal, and the Olympics couldn't be over. I just wouldn't accept that my dream had ended.

It would be a lie to say that I thought of Terry in those first few days in the hospital bed in Germany; I didn't. I was confused, I was angry, I was shocked, but I was also determined. Nobody knew me like I did, and they didn't know what my body was capable of. I knew I could get to the Olympic Games that year, and I gave that goal everything in my power despite the odds and in spite of all the people who told me, however kindly, to give it up. I made it to those Olympics and came home with a bronze medal for Canada.

That is how I relate to Terry most strongly. I imagine he must have had the same desire to be self-determining, to do what was in his head and heart regardless of how many people thought it was impossible, preposterous, dangerous, or at best ill-advised.

Truly great accomplishments are usually the product of magical thinking. Part of why we still remember and celebrate Terry is because he had the ability to imagine the future, to see beyond his current circumstance, and to commit to giving his best effort. It is people who think like Terry that go on to do big things: they refuse to be defined by limitations. They reject the belief that change is impossible, and they push against the crushing apathy of modern times. Terry challenged us to care about something, to be bigger than we think we are, and to say no to anything that threatens to make us small. Terry challenged us to find our courage individually, and collectively as a nation, to do our own great things.

Terry's Marathon of Hope was about finding a cure for cancer, but it became so much more. The concept of raising awareness and money by physically challenging yourself in such a public way was totally new at the time. He created a genre of giving, going from town to town across this huge country, collecting dollar by dollar. In doing so, Terry proved that one individual can truly make a difference. The Terry Fox Run created a national movement around giving, and thousands have benefitted from it.

All of my four kids have participated and fundraised for the Terry Fox Run. When they learned about Terry in school, it was interesting to witness how a man they never met, a young man who died so long ago while living out his dream, was able to inspire and captivate them. That same inspiration is sparked every year across Canada and around the world as our children discover the truly remarkable young man he was.

A few years ago, I went to the Terry Fox Marathon of Hope exhibit in Victoria. As I looked at his worn shoes, torn shirt, and the van that housed Terry and his friends, I experienced the same thrill and deep pride I've felt each time I encounter Terry's story. Forty years after seeing him in Nathan Phillips Square, Terry and the example he set for us still moves me in big ways. I feel Terry's influence right down to my soul; I don't particularly remember the words he said that day in Toronto, but I remember how he made, and still makes, me feel—as if I can do anything I set my mind to. And because I can, I should. And so, with gratitude to Terry, that's what I continue to do.

Thanks to Terry, I am still living with my cancer and am able to visit Terry Fox Plaza each time I get to Vancouver.

Darrin Park

DARRIN PARK IS a husband, father, junior high school teacher, and life member of the Kinsmen Club of Edmonton. He is living with cancer and has been the organizer for the Terry Fox Run in Edmonton since 2015.

My path to becoming a volunteer for the Terry Fox Foundation, one of the most fulfilling experiences of my life, came from horrific circumstances. I had been a teacher for twenty-one years when I suffered a sudden seizure. After I was rushed to the emergency room, the doctor discovered that I had a large brain tumour and told me I had less than two years to live. Many weeks later, the tumour was diagnosed as a rare form of cancer, and I was admitted to Edmonton's Cross Cancer Institute. At the time, I was only the third person in North America living with this particular type of cancer and the fourth ever in Alberta. My prognosis was grim. The doctors didn't have a set treatment for me, and even if I did make it through the treatment (which I was told was highly unlikely), my life expectancy was just over a year at most. I told the medical team to hit me as hard as they could and I would deal with it.

Terry has always been a hero to me, even before I was diagnosed with cancer. I was in the seventh grade when Terry was running the Marathon of Hope and I remember watching him on TV. When my treatments were at their worst, I thought of Terry and of what he had endured. His perseverance motivated and inspired me to get through my treatment. Although my chemo treatments were horrible, I made it. Cancer is such an awful disease. I would never want anyone to have to go through it, but like Terry taught us, you have to look at and focus on the positive.

My cancer has left me living with pain every day and with a lack of dexterity. If I am walking and one of my legs isn't cooperating, or if my fingers quit working, or if the pain becomes too intense, I hold in my hand a Terry Fox loonie that I always carry with me. It reminds me of him and what he endured. It gets me through each day.

During my five months in the Cross Cancer Institute, many of my former students, colleagues, friends, and family were donating money in my name to different charities supporting cancer research. I have always been involved in volunteer work with my schools, community, service clubs, and charities, so I looked into where money donated to cancer foundations actually goes. Through all my research, the Terry Fox Foundation emerged as the best, always coming up at the top of the list. Every Terry Fox Run is 100 percent organized and executed by volunteers. That is why close to eighty cents of each dollar raised for the Terry Fox Foundation goes directly to cancer research. This discovery was the trigger and catalyst I needed. As I was no longer able to continue working as a teacher, I asked to be involved with the Terry Fox Foundation,

and I'm now beginning my sixth year as the run organizer for
the Terry Fox Run in Edmonton.

There were two research projects funded by the Terry Fox
Foundation that resulted in part of my cancer treatment. If
Terry hadn't decided to run, or if his family had not embedded
his values into the Terry Fox Foundation, I would not be alive
today. When people describe Terry, traits like motivated, courageous, inspiring, and selfless always come up, and he was all
those and more. To me, however, tenacity and resilience are
my connection to Terry—learning to deal with what life throws
at you, continuing to get up each day and do your best. I am
so thankful to wake up each and every day, and that would not
have been possible without Terry.

In my role as a Terry Fox Foundation volunteer, I have
the opportunity to speak at schools, service club meetings,
business luncheons, and conferences across Canada about my
cancer experience and Terry Fox. When I speak, I try to share
those aspects of Terry: how his example teaches each of us how
to survive and overcome obstacles while remaining positive,
even in the direst of circumstances. In all my years of speaking, I have never heard a negative word about Terry Fox. I like
to show people a picture of Terry and ask them to tell me who
they see. In six years of doing this, not a single person has said
"Terry Fox" without a big smile and glowing vibrant emotion.
This reaction is one of the reasons why I am so engaged and
committed to volunteering with the foundation. Forty years
after the Marathon of Hope, Terry Fox's spirit and legacy is
alive, strong, and still gaining momentum. He brought an

entire country together, he united us all, and he will always make us proud to be Canadian.

I do not believe there has ever been or will ever be another Canadian who could do what Terry Fox did. An unknown twenty-one-year-old with one leg, who only wanted to rid the world of a horrific disease that continues to have the highest death rate in Canada every year. He did not want fame, fortune, or recognition; he always said he was equal to every one of us, no better or no worse. Terry Fox taught us that together we can outrun cancer. That together we can achieve the seemingly impossible. We are so much better because of him. I know I am.

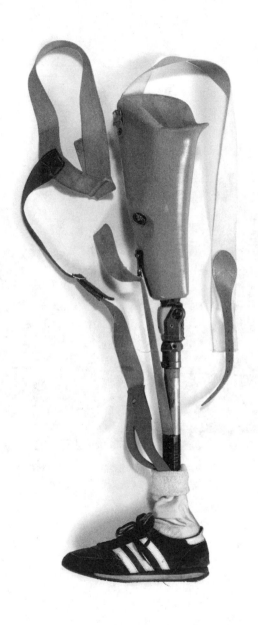

He brought our country together, and put us all on the same team.

Christine Sinclair

BORN IN BURNABY, B.C., Christine Sinclair is Canada's most renowned soccer player. As captain of the Canadian national team, she has won two bronze medals at the Olympics, been appointed an officer of the Order of Canada, and became the world's all-time leading goal scorer for both men and women in 2020. Christine currently plays professionally for the Portland Thorns in the National Women's Soccer League.

The togetherness aspect of team sports is what drives me. I love that so many people can put their egos aside to help the team be better, to achieve something as one, to win and lose side by side. During my highs and lows, I find motivation to keep going in the knowledge that my teammates are training alongside me. I never want to let anyone down. That being said, in a strange way, being part of a team takes the pressure off me as an individual player. It's one of the biggest reasons I chose a team sport; when I was growing up, I ran cross-country for a while but couldn't handle the stress it gave me. When I think of Terry's goal to run across the country, which is crazy in the best way possible, I'm even more astounded that he set out to do it alone. He was obviously such a strong young man to make that decision and to sacrifice so much of himself.

As an athlete, I know what it feels like when people pay attention to your performance at big events, like the Olympic Games or the World Cup, or to how your professional team fares over the course of a season. But I think it's easy for people to overlook the hours, months, and years of training that athletes put in to get there. Those unseen moments for an athlete amount to more than any one event, because what matters most is how hard you work behind the scenes. The way Terry ran when the media wasn't following him or even cared about what he was doing, particularly at the beginning of his run, says everything you need to know about him as an athlete. His inner drive was tremendous. Certain people find it exciting to give their absolute all, to never take shortcuts, and to grind it out. Given the willingness he showed to keep going day after day, Terry must have been one of those people. He was determined to prove the doubters wrong.

I read something recently about the late basketball player Kobe Bryant and it hit me hard. At his jersey-retirement ceremony a few years ago, he told his daughters that if you work hard enough, dreams come true. What he hoped they knew beyond that was "those times when you get up early and you work hard, those times when you stay up late and you work hard, those times when you don't feel like working—you're too tired, you don't want to push yourself—but you do it anyway: that is actually the dream. It's not the destination, it's the journey." That spoke to me because I don't remember the details of all the games I've played in, but the grind has always felt exciting to me. I have no regrets about how anything turned out because I've given my all. I hope Terry felt the same way. He may not have reached British Columbia, but every morning when he stepped foot on the highway and began his run, he made his dream come true.

Enjoying the journey is something I'm focused on now more than ever. When my father passed away from cancer four years ago, I realized how precious time is. I'm trying to not take any moments for granted, and I'm doing my best to let go of things that used to stress me out. And when I think of how young Terry was when he was diagnosed with cancer, I am inspired by his courage. There were so many obstacles on his journey and yet he faced his adversity with grace. He was kind and humble, even when fame eventually found him. I'm sure that wasn't a choice: it was just who he was as a person. Terry's humility left a lasting impression on our entire country. To me, he'll always be the rarest bright light, a young man who shone bravely and quietly, even when no one was watching.

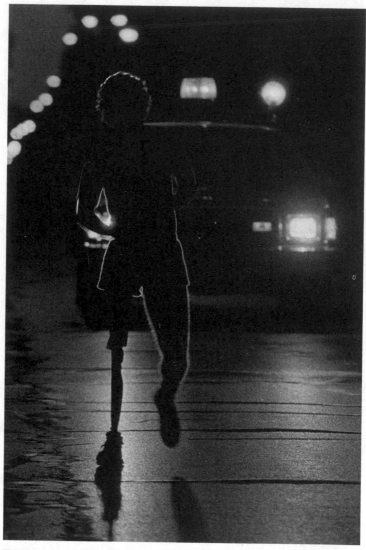

The photo I see every time I leave my house, one that provides constant inspiration to be determined and maintain my work ethic, even on the most difficult days.

Sidney Crosby

BORN AND RAISED in Nova Scotia, Sidney Crosby is one of the most accomplished hockey players of all time. As captain of the Pittsburgh Penguins in the National Hockey League, he has won three Stanley Cups, two Hart Memorial Trophies, and two Conn Smythe Trophies, among other awards. As part of Team Canada, he has won gold at two Olympic Games. Sidney lives in Sewickley, Pennsylvania, and often returns to Cole Harbour, his hometown.

In the entryway of my house, I have a framed photo of Terry Fox hanging on the wall. Terry is running in the dark and a car is following him, its headlights making him a silhouette. I'd seen that picture many times growing up. It stuck with me, so when I moved into my house about seven years ago, I found it online and bought it. I've always liked having inspirational quotes up at the different places I've lived, and the quote from Terry at the bottom of the picture really resonates with me. It says, "Today, we got up at 4:00 a.m. As usual, it was tough." His words are a reminder that not every day is going to be great or easy, but your work ethic and commitment will get you through.

When you're growing up and trying to find your way, you look for role models. They come in different forms, family members, friends, or other athletes, they are people who inspire you. My parents are very hard-working people. They instilled in me the importance of having a strong work ethic and a purpose. They taught me to give my best in school, sports, and everything else, and I've tried to keep that in mind throughout my life. When I learned about Terry, I admired him right away. The mindset he had to say, "I have this adversity, but I'm going to try to create awareness and make something good come of it," impressed me at a young age. He knew the road would be tough but he travelled it anyway.

I remember learning a lot about him in school, whether it was watching a video about his story, doing group projects, or fundraising for the Terry Fox Run every September. His outlook was amazing, especially for someone so young. He also made me realize just how fortunate I am to be healthy. You don't have to be an athlete to appreciate the way he handled things when he was diagnosed with cancer. He was one of my biggest heroes, not just for trying to run across Canada but because of the way he carried himself. Looking back on my school days, I'm grateful they gave me someone like him to respect and admire. And I'm so happy kids today still learn about him. Working hard, being humble, and helping others are such important qualities for young people to learn about and strive to foster in themselves. Terry wanted to be a good example for others and help them face their own challenging circumstances.

Unfortunately, cancer is something we can all relate to. It's touched all of our lives in one way or another. I've lost both my grandmothers to cancer, and over the years, I've spent time with kids and adults who are fighting through it. Terry's goal was to find a cure and beat cancer. I believe everyone can play a part in fulfilling his dream. We can raise money, attend his run, and share his story with others. We can come together in smaller ways, too. Whether it's encouraging someone who's dealing with cancer or taking their mind off things for a while, the important thing is recognizing what others are going through and doing our best to help each other out.

Terry was the ultimate example of putting others first. When he was faced with a daunting personal diagnosis and saw kids who were suffering, he decided to do something for the collective good. No one can match the impact he's had. A few years ago, British Columbians voted on the province's best moment in sports history. Deservedly, Terry's Marathon of Hope won. People voted for him over notable moments in sports of all kinds, including my own "Golden Goal" at the 2010 Olympics. It was nice to be included in that group, but I would never put myself close to the same level as Terry. What he did for cancer research— not to mention the mental strength, perseverance, and courage he showed on his run—was unheard of. Nobody would have blamed him for stopping, yet he kept going. He was unbelievable.

The Canadian players who come to my house know who Terry was and what he stood for. And if someone comes over, sees the picture, and asks who Terry Fox was, I'm pretty happy and proud to tell his story. He has made a difference in so many people's lives, including mine. Every time I pass that picture of him, he motivates me to be a better player and a better person. You couldn't ask for more from a role model.

Participating in an Australia Terry Fox Run was so moving—Terry's influence has travelled across oceans.

Debbie Laurie

BORN AND RAISED in Quebec City, Debbie taught math, science, history, geography, and English at Riverview School in Port-Cartier, Quebec. In recognition of her involvement with the Terry Fox Foundation, she was a torchbearer in the 2010 Vancouver Olympics torch relay. Debbie retired in 2013 but remains very active as a volunteer.

I remember the Saturday Terry started his Marathon of Hope. I was in my second year of teaching high school math, just three days shy of my twenty-fourth birthday. News began trickling out of Newfoundland, and the curly-haired, one-legged young man running along a highway—sometimes grinning, sometimes grimacing—captivated my heart and soul. Four years earlier, I had lost my dad to lung cancer at the age of forty-three. Terry had my support and admiration. I eagerly collected newspaper clippings about his journey and watched him on the evening news. Before I knew it, the school year had ended, Terry had reached Montreal, support for his run was building in Ontario, summer had flown by, and then September 1 arrived.

It was Labour Day Monday and I saw Terry on the news, climbing into the van. They said he was going to the hospital for tests. X-rays revealed what no one wanted to hear. "But all I can say is that if there's any way I can get out there again and finish it, I will." Terry's words played over and over in my head, as I watched him being lifted into a jet to fly home. They still haunt me.

That Sunday, CTV held a national telethon in Terry's name, and host Lloyd Robertson suggested folks get out there and do something spontaneous. Fellow teacher Mary Cormier, my dear friend Donna Paul, and I organized a walk the next Saturday. We created pledge sheets and had hoodies made at a local sports store. Fourteen students showed up and the first Terry Fox Run was held, a year before the annual runs began. We raised $1,200 and I had found a new focus in life. In Port-Cartier, I am now affectionately known as Madame Terry Fox, as I organized the runs for thirty-three years. I am proud to say that Riverview School has walked every year since 1980 with September 2019 being our fortieth.

Ten years ago, I purchased a Terry Fox flag and felt that it needed a purpose other than being displayed during the annual runs. As I neared retirement and was bitten by the travel bug, I decided that I would bring it with me. I planned to travel the world and share his inspirational message, and a symbol of Terry would travel alongside me.

The flag made its maiden journey to Zermatt, Switzerland, to the peak of the Matterhorn. No sooner did I have it out of my backpack when a couple from Toronto gasped, "Oh my God, that's Terry Fox!" In Rome, it was blessed by Pope Benedict XVI in St. Peter's Square. On a flight from Montreal to Calgary in 2014, former prime minister Brian Mulroney posed for a photo with it. It's been to Kenya where it sailed high above the Maasai Mara in a hot-air balloon and rode on a camel on the beach in Mombasa; it's travelled to South Africa where it went on safari in Kruger National Park and out to Robben Island where Nelson Mandela was imprisoned.

In September 2016, I took the flag with me to Namibia. I was excited for the trip, but it marked the first time I wouldn't be in Canada on the day of the Terry Fox Run. I sought a challenge worthy of Terry, and our local guide suggested climbing Big Daddy, the highest sand dune in Namib-Naukluft National Park. With the flag on my shoulder, I headed for the base of the dune under the scorching sun. Ahead of me was a fellow on crutches also heading toward the dune; he only had one leg. I asked if he knew who Terry was, gave him a quick bio, and learned that since losing his leg, it had been his dream to climb this dune. He and his parents had come from Belgium to do so. His tenacity and dedication to his goal reminded me so much of Terry, and it brought to mind one of his famous quotes: "Dreams are made possible if you try." Though our paths never crossed again, I hope my fellow climber realized his dream.

A year later, I embarked on my first Australian adventure. There I met one of the most inspirational Terry Foxers: Matthew Reid is a city transit driver with a big dream—that all children in Australia know who Terry Fox is. He organized a Terry Fox Run in 2018, and I promised to return for the next one!

The following year, I flew back to keep that promise. But first I went on a bus tour from Melbourne to Adelaide. The tour director, Delma, had been taking photos of me with my flag and was curious about the young man on it. At her request, I addressed the other coach passengers to tell them about Terry. Fifteen minutes later, she was crying and the rest of the passengers were applauding. I was brought to tears the next day when I learned they had all donated to the run. Folks thanked me for sharing Terry's story, saying they would never forget him.

In Sydney, Matthew gave me a tour of the run's route. I was moved to see Terry's name and image on the beautiful Terry Fox Run Australia banners on park fences, schoolyard entrances, and local businesses. Matthew is an incredible one-man organizing machine; 200 people participated in the 2019 run, and I was really impressed to see so many families participating. All monies raised went to local pediatric cancer research. I am sure Terry would have been impressed by what Matthew has accomplished. As Christie Blatchford wrote, "He gave us a dream as big as our country," and Terry's dream has spread far beyond our borders.

I feel blessed to share the message of that grinning, curly-haired, one-legged young man running along the highway four decades ago. Similar to Terry, ". . . right now I can look back and think of all the good things that happened and the good people I met . . ." Thank you, Terry, for inspiring me then and every day since.

The inscription on the Terry Fox memorial in Thunder Bay inspired me and reminded me that I must leave my mark and help make the world a better place.

Catriona Le May Doan

BORN IN SASKATOON, Saskatchewan, Catriona Le May Doan, O.C., is a two-time Olympic champion and five-time World Champion in long track speed skating. She is a Gemini-winning broadcaster, highly-sought-after motivational speaker, member of Canada's Sports Hall of Fame, and an officer of the Order of Canada. She currently lives in Calgary with her children, Greta and Easton.

I remember watching Terry on television—seeing images of him grimacing through painful strides. Running through weather that would keep most of us inside. In his iconic T-shirt, shorts, and blue sneakers that became so familiar to us.

I didn't understand why a young guy—but one who seemed *so* much older than my nine-year-old self—would do this. Terry wasn't doing the run for himself. He wasn't pushing his body to get better and improve his performance for himself. He was doing it for others. I wasn't able to comprehend the whys of his goal, why he was running. I was just a kid.

What I came to understand, many years later, is that Terry was also just a kid.

Back then, I heard about him wanting to help others so they would not suffer the way he had. I was too young to understand how Terry running a marathon every day was going to help.

Terry was doing his run when I first started speed skating. Speed skating in Saskatoon was, and still is, not easy. It means being outside in freezing temperatures skating in spandex, going around and around, and only turning left. We used to layer on a few pairs of long underwear, as well as coats, big mitts, and a neck warmer—pulled up as far as it would go— and paste Vaseline on any exposed skin to prevent frostbite.

That was the training routine night after night. We kept at it, determined to fulfill our own performance goals. I had goals for myself: to qualify for the Canada Games, for the national team, for the Olympics. Ultimately, my dream was to stand on top of the Olympic podium. It took me a very long time to understand that what had driven Terry toward his goal with his Marathon of Hope was very different from what motivated me as I pushed myself toward my personal goals. Terry's goal was always about others.

It took me becoming a mum to understand the purpose of Terry's run. It took me loving others so much, unconditionally and wanting to make sure that they were protected, to understand what Terry did. But Terry wasn't a dad. He didn't have kids. Terry just gave himself to others selflessly because that's who he was.

I am often asked why I committed so many years to speed skating. Why I gave my time and energy to going around and around on an oval. I put a lot of life milestones on hold, including going to post-secondary school, having kids, and living what is considered a "normal" life. I did it because I was chasing the perfect race. High-performance athletes live in a performance bubble, and I am stubborn. I never raced the perfect race—the perfect race doesn't exist—but I believe I came as close as I could. And along the way, inspired by great Canadian leaders like Terry, I pushed myself farther than I thought possible, physically, emotionally, and mentally.

I used to wear dark glasses when I raced. Most people think it was to make me look tough, but it was so no one could see the fear in my eyes. After a fall at the Olympic Games in 1994, I took a long time to recover emotionally, learning about myself and my value as I prepared for Nagano. And finally, on February 14, 1998, and in just over 37 seconds, I realized my childhood dream. That day, I sang our national anthem from the top of the Olympic podium.

I knew Salt Lake City would be my last Olympic Games. At that point, no Canadian individual had ever won back-to-back gold medals at the Olympics. On February 14, 2002, four years after my first gold medal, I stood on the very top of the podium again. In this success, I broke down barriers and paved a way for other Canadians to discover their dreams in life and sport. After I stepped out of my performance bubble, I committed my life to giving back.

None of this would have been possible if I didn't have a hero like Terry to look up to, to demonstrate how to push yourself farther that you thought possible. I doubt Terry could have imagined that forty years after he ran across our great country, his legacy would be so immense and that he would continue to have a positive impact on so many in Canada and around the world. He has given us so much.

I imagine how proud Betty Fox was of her son Terry. Yes, she raised a stubborn son, one who was so determined, who was not considered naturally athletic, but who had an exceptional work ethic. Most impressive and most important of all, she raised a son who cared more for others than himself.

I was recently in Thunder Bay and finally saw the Terry Fox monument there. Seeing the statue of Terry was emotional and inspiring. His quote is etched in stone: "Dreams are made if people only try. I believe in miracles . . . I have to . . . Because somewhere the hurting must stop." That is where he physically ended his run. While it may be his finish line, it is more importantly the beginning of his incredible legacy.

At the base of the statue are these powerful words: "To every Canadian. He left us his challenge—a challenge each of us will meet in our own way."

Thank you, Terry. Thank you for challenging me. Thank you for being an example to me. Though we are on this Earth for just a brief period of time, it is during that time that we must make a mark. A mark on others. A mark on our community. A mark that will inspire at least one person to be better and achieve more than they ever thought possible.

Thank you, Terry, for being my hero.

Terry testing himself in September, 1979, by running the Prince George to Boston marathon.

Discussing what drove the unrelenting pursuit of his dream with the young man brimming over with hope and purpose, June 1980.

Leslie Scrivener

LESLIE SCRIVENER IS a former *Toronto Star* feature writer. She is the author of *Terry Fox: His Story* and holds a master of journalism degree from the University of Western Ontario.

———————————

The idea to run across Canada came to Terry Fox the night before his leg was amputated, when he read about a one-legged runner competing in the Boston Marathon. It was a dream or a fantasy, he said. Something wildly improbable, something a teenager would think of on the eve of the gravest crisis of his life.

Who would he be after he lost his leg? What could he do? He kept this dream to himself for a long time and set about rebuilding his life and his identity as a young athlete. Terry played golf with his father, Rolly, and later wheelchair basketball while undergoing chemotherapy. He was skeletally thin, had lost his hair, and sometimes was so tired that he fell asleep on the sidelines during games.

He had always pushed himself and often resisted the discouraging voice of adult reason, the way young people do. As a boy, Terry loved basketball but showed scant talent for the game and his coach urged him to consider other sports.

Besides, he was small and there were more gifted players. Somehow he made the team (already showing that spirit of never giving up), though he was the worst player. He had one minute of floor time that first season in middle school. But he practised relentlessly, and by the time he got to university, he was good enough for the junior varsity team.

In 1979, two years after his operation, Terry started running on a track near his house and the struggle nearly did him in. First one-quarter of a mile, then a half, then a full mile. Sometimes his stump rubbed raw where it met the bucket of the artificial leg and blood streamed down, soaking his socks.

But he was making progress, felt the rewards, and was already unstoppable. So it wasn't surprising, in hindsight, that when Terry broke the news to his mother, Betty—that he was training for a cross-Canada run—they shouted at each other and she said he was not going to do it and he said he was and she said it was a stupid idea and he said he was going to do it anyway. And then he stormed out, slamming the door behind him.

This is to say that there were many occasions when Terry, who was easy to get along with, resisted the advice of his elders who really did know better. He pursued his dream with the laser focus of the young. It's only crazy until you do it, as the Nike slogan goes.

The Canadian Cancer Society was doubtful about sponsoring him. He was told to go away and get some backers; those at the society thought they would likely not hear from him again. To their surprise, he gained support from big-name corporations.

His doctor told him his heart may not withstand the rigours of long, daily runs and didn't want him to go. If Terry showed any signs of dizziness or shortness of breath, he was to stop. Terry ignored that advice, too. He had already experienced those symptoms, but he kept that to himself. Later, when he was running through the Maritimes, the Canadian Cancer Society ordered him to have a medical checkup. He refused.

And so it went. A young man doing what he had to do.

What drove him? As a teenager undergoing cancer treatment, he had listened as doctors told children they had a 15 percent chance of living, and he'd heard their pleas for help. "I had to do something about it," he said. There was an urgent need, so he couldn't waste time. What he could do, as a young man, was run. And to make the task even more challenging, he was going to run into the wind, from east to west. He wanted to prove that he, someone who seemed to have outrun cancer, was worthy of this wonderful new life.

He stood on picnic tables and park benches when called on to speak, but they weren't soapboxes and he didn't present himself as an activist for disability rights or cancer research. He embodied those causes. He didn't intellectualize but told his story in the clearest, most natural way. He was an unusually gifted communicator, and his answers to reporters' questions were thoughtful and meaningful.

His example led to change. He refused to a wear a corporate logo, long before that became a stance athletes took. In running shorts, he exposed the simple prosthetic leg he wore. Amputee runners have since said that because of Terry, they didn't feel so self-conscious and didn't hide their artificial limbs.

As for the running, his achievement was unmatched: an amputee running a marathon, averaging twenty-six miles a day, for 143 days. Running seemed like a torment to people who saw him—the look on his face!—but to hear Terry tell it, he was having the time of his life, doing exactly what he wanted. It was one wonderful adventure, he said. One more thing older folks didn't get.

Forty years later, not a day goes by in which I do not think of Terry. What do I remember from that summer of 1980? He was so young and brimming with hope. He loved the first run of the day, when it was cool and still dark, before anything could go wrong, before he was pestered by journalists who thought it was a great story to run with him or before he was told that he had to make an important detour to talk to a fundraiser. How his little brother Darrell and best pal Doug Alward—his band of brothers—were tender in their service. How he wore the map of Canada on his shirt. How small and solitary he looked—just a kid—as he toiled along small-town main streets and two-lane highways. The boldness of his dream and the tragic price he paid. In the end, it cost him his life, but as you watched him do it, it seemed the right thing, the thing you would always remember.

The cap Terry wore after losing his hair during chemo treatments. He once confided to his family that losing his hair was almost as difficult as losing his leg.

The toughest man, who made the best of a poor situation and changed our country forever. Here, wearing the insignia of the Order of Canada.

Afterword

Karl Subban

KARL SUBBAN IS a retired schoolteacher and administrator of thirty years with the Toronto District School Board. He worked with Canadian Tire on a project that teaches Canadian families about the benefits of their children participating in hockey, and he served as an ambassador for Hyundai Hockey Helpers Program. When Karl is not delivering empowering speeches to Canadian audiences on how to find one's potential, he spends time teaching his grandchildren how to skate.

From the backyard hockey rink to the nail-biting suspense of draft days, Karl Subban's memoir How We Did It *mixes personal stories with lessons he learned as a father, coach, and principal. Dedicated to helping everyone believe in and achieve their full potential, Karl describes one of the people he has drawn inspiration from—Terry Fox.*

Your university years are tough. They test you not only as a scholar but as a person. To succeed you need to seek out inspiration from the lives of those you look up to. One of those people during my time in Thunder Bay was someone I never had the chance to meet: Terry Fox. Terry and I were born in the same year, 1958. Terry was at Simon Fraser University when I was at Lakehead, and he had been a basketball player, too. I thought we had a lot in common. In 1980, I followed his cross-country Marathon of Hope, a journey he undertook to raise money to fight cancer. And when his run ended just outside Thunder Bay, it was very emotional for me. All Canadians were awed by his courage. We wanted to be part of his mission, and people across the country lined the highways to see him, to show him that he wasn't alone.

I'll never forget the first time I visited the Terry Fox monument just outside Thunder Bay. It has since been moved to higher ground above the highway and is adjacent to a rest stop and more parking, but when I first saw his statue, it stood right beside the Trans-Canada Highway, overlooking the dense forest that spreads out down to the shores of Lake Superior. I could feel the power of the man there.

Terry provided many memorable quotes, but there is one that stands out for me, something he said after being asked how he managed to run a marathon every day: "I just kept running to the next telephone pole and when I got there I would focus on the next pole." He dreamed big but he took small steps—which he had to do because of his artificial right leg—one pole to the next. It's an approach we can all learn from when we set out to accomplish our dreams. Terry Fox's Marathon of Hope may have ended in Thunder Bay, but his dream did not die there. Through his foundation, it has lived on and grown larger, passing on to new generations who keep his name and cause alive.

Excerpted from How We Did It *by Karl Subban and Scott Colby.*

One of the last photos taken of Terry, December 1980. A big Dolly Parton fan, in the early days of the Marathon Terry would listen to her music after completing his run for the day.

The gold album we presented to Terry—it's one of our greatest honours that our music accompanied the Marathon of Hope.

Epilogue

Geddy Lee

GEDDY LEE IS an award-winning musician, best known as the lead singer, bassist, and keyboardist of Rush, a Canadian rock band. In 1996, Geddy and his bandmates, Alex Lifeson and Neil Peart, became officers of the Order of Canada, the first band to be honoured as a group. Geddy lives in Toronto with his wife, Nancy.

In the fall of 1980, our band sent Terry a gold album commemorating the sale of more than 50,000 units of *Permanent Waves*, the album we'd released earlier that year. I'm afraid I don't recall exactly who initiated that gift, probably our manager Ray Danniels, but of course we all followed Terry's Marathon of Hope with great interest, and we were all too happy to recognize him in any way we could. I understand music was very much a part of the Marathon of Hope, and though the guys' music interests varied, Rush was there during Terry's run. Just knowing that our music might have made even one day more manageable for Terry is deeply meaningful. Terry gave the world so much, and if we could offer him even the slightest bit of encouragement or joy, that was all we wanted. When he was back at home, we heard he wasn't doing well and hoped sending him our album would lift his spirits. It was the stuff of legends: a fellow of his age enduring the struggles he had with such bravery and selflessness. As fellow Canadians, we were extremely proud of him.

We all felt that Terry's dedication was something special—and his monumental run continues to inspire today. Hearing my five-year-old grandson tell me about how he just ran in the annual Terry Fox Run at his school made me stop to realize how the legend of Terry Fox just keeps on growing, and we are witness to yet another generation being inspired by this real-life hero. To me, this speaks volumes about our country's values and Terry's legacy.

Of course, the recent passing of my friend and bandmate, Neil Peart, was a very painful reminder of how important funding is for all types of cancer research. Our loss is the world's loss, and we are but one family out of so many that have had to go through this kind of ordeal. The need to fight this disease continues, and the name Terry Fox continues to inspire. I'm heartened by the fact that forty years after the Marathon of Hope, we are all still running for Terry. May we never stop.

Words from Terry

October 15, 1979

Dear Sir;

My name is Terry Fox, I am 21 years old, and I am an amputee. I lost my right leg two and a half years ago due to cancer.

The night before my amputation, my former basketball coach brought me a magazine with an article on an amputee who ran in the New York Marathon. It was then when I decided to meet this new challenge head on and not only overcome my disability, but conquer it in such a way that I could never look back and say it disabled me. But I soon realized that that would only be half my quest, for as I went through the 16 months of the physically and emotionally draining ordeal of chemotherapy, I was rudely awakened by the feelings that surrounded and coursed throughout the Cancer Clinic. There were the faces with the brave smiles, and the ones who had given up smiling. There were the feelings of hopeful denial, and the feelings of despair. My quest would not be a selfish one. I could not leave knowing these faces and feelings would still exist, even though I would be set free from mine. Somewhere the hurting must stop... and I was determined to take myself to the limit for this cause.

I feel now is the time to make good my promise. I have been training for 8 months, running on an artificial leg. Starting with ½ mile, I have now worked up to 13½ miles a day, adding a half mile weekly.

Form the beginning the going was extremely difficult, and I was facing chronic ailments foriegn to runners with two legs, in addition to the common physical strains felt by all dedicated athletes. But these problems are now behind me, as I have either out-persisted or learned to deal with them. I feel strong not only physically, but more important, emotionally. Soon I will be adding one full mile each week, and coupled with the weight training I have been doing three times a week, by April next year I will be ready to achieve something that for me was once only a distant dream reserved for the world of miracles; to run across Canada to raise money for the fight against cancer.

October 15, 1979, a letter Terry sent to the B.C. Division of the Canadian Cancer Society asking for support on his run.

The running I can do, even if I have to crawl every last mile. But there are some barriers I cannot overcome alone. I need your help, your sponsorship, to provide the means to sustain myself and two others who have consented to put aside those 5 months to be my companions and aides. We will need transportation to Newfoundland, a camper-type vehicle to meet us there, and money for food, gas and other necessities. My three years in university have quite aptly drained me financially, and just the thought that I will require 26 pairs of running shoes for myself and running companion makes my now dwindling account crawl deeper into it's hole.

Please consider my plea carefully, and notify me if you come to any decisions, good or bad. My number is listed below and a message can be left at my home any time of the day.

We need your help. The people in cancer clinics all over the world need people who believe in miracles. I'm not a dreamer, and I'm not saying that this will initiate any kind of definitive answer or cure to cancer, but I believe in miracles. I have to.

Yours Sincerely,

Address 3337 MORRILL ST
P. COQUITLAM V3B 4M4   Terry Fox

phone: 464-5652

Mrs B. Fox   References

Blair MacKenzie
Executive Director, Canadian Cancer Society
B.C. and Yukon Division
1926 West Broadway
736-1211

Colin B. Johnstone
Coordinating Chaplain, Cancer Control Agency of B.C.
2656 Heather Street, Vancouver, B.C.
V5Z-3J3
873-6212 (local 327)

This book would not have been possible without the Fox family; pictured here, as children, Terry, Darrell, Fred, and Judith.

Acknowledgments

WHEN WE EMBARKED on this project, we hoped that a collection of memories, stories, letters, and anecdotes expressing what Terry Fox means to Canadians far and wide would be a fitting way to mark the fortieth anniversary of the Marathon of Hope. We thought the responses would be positive, but we could never have anticipated the overwhelming level of enthusiasm our requests were met with. Each response we received was overflowing with gratitude and love for Terry. Gathering each letter for this collection has been inspiring, humbling, and fulfilling; knowing that Terry's legacy is dear to so many encourages us to continue his dream. This collection provides just a glimpse of Terry's profound impact. But those who have taken the time to share their thoughts have found words that will resonate with readers' own feelings beautifully. The book team would like to thank each and every contributor for their incredible openness to share these emotional stories. Your willingness to pass on your memories and inspiration is one of the many reasons why Terry's legacy endures still.

We had outstanding help reaching these phenomenal contributors, and this collection would not have been possible without gracious colleagues and friends who helped us get in touch with contributors. For their aid, we thank Andy McCreath, Pamela Murray, Leslie Gallacher, Jeffrey Latimer,

Bhavna Chauhan, Brian Levine, and Bill Vigars. We are grateful to Les Potapczyk for his invaluable help tracking down photographs we were afraid had been lost, and Gail Harvey for the use of her iconic photographs. Many friends assisted in reaching our contributors, and numerous people (including John Danakas, Mary Beth Leatherdale, and Nancy Tinari) helped write the letters—for this, we thank you.

Many members of the Terry Fox Foundation contributed to this project by sourcing photographs, tracking down volunteers, and spreading the word. We thank everyone at the foundation, Wendy Kennelly and Gwen Smith-Walsh in particular. Ara Sahakian, interim executive director of the Terry Fox Foundation, has been an unwavering leader in spearheading not only this project but also many additional fortieth-anniversary initiatives.

Our deepest gratitude to James McCreath, for his incredible idea and unflagging work on this collection. He both conceived of this project and worked tirelessly to find contributors and put the pieces together. James would like to thank his parents, Grit and Scott McCreath, for taking their three-year-old to the first-ever Terry Fox Run in 1981. It sparked a lifelong veneration for Terry's bravery. Kirstie McLellan Day was instrumental in connecting the Terry Fox Foundation with Penguin Random House Canada to collaborate on this monumental collection.

Our unflappable writer, Michelle Magnan McIvor, for her expertise in guiding experiences and memories of Terry to the page. Michelle likes to note that being part of *Forever Terry* has been one of her greatest honours, but this collection would not have been possible without her and, truly, having her on board is one of *our* greatest honours. Michelle would like to thank her husband, Cameron, and their children, Hudson and Marlowe, for their inspiration.

Our passionate and championing editor Nicholas Garrison, who provided invaluable vision, direction, and commentary throughout. He never wavered from his vision of cementing these stories so as to convey Terry's enduring legacy for generations to come and to capture memories of Terry on paper in a new way. Our deadline- and detail-oriented editor Alanna McMullen, for keeping the many moving parts on track. Crissy Calhoun, for her careful and thorough copy edit and for always saying "yes!" when we asked yet one last favour of her. Terri Nimmo, Penguin Random House's invaluable creative design director, for the elegant and timeless design of this book and its cover.

Our everlasting appreciation goes to the Fox family for their willingness to give Canadians yet another opportunity to love and understand Terry's remarkable legacy. Darrell Fox has been exceedingly generous with his time, expertise, and support. His careful curation of this collection has ensured the widest range of perspectives. Darrell hates being praised and this note will embarrass him to no end, but we are forever grateful for everything he has done both for this project and to promote the legacy of Terry Fox. We know that Terry would be so proud of the way his family has carried on his dream.

A short break from running to share his story in Ottawa.

Photo Credits

Page i: © Bettmann, Getty Images

Page ii: © Gail Harvey

Page viii: courtesy of the Fox family

Page 10: © Marlene North

Page 13: © Gail Harvey

Page 14: courtesy of the Fox family

Page 20: © David Cooper / *Toronto Star*, Getty Images

Page 25: © Canadian Museum of History,
    IMG2015-0290-0003-Dm

Page 26: © Ed Linkewich

Page 31: © Jim McKnight

Page 32: credit unknown

Page 37: © *Quebec Chronicle-Telegraph*

Page 38: courtesy of the Fox family

Page 42: © Donna L. Ball

Page 48: © David Cooper / *Toronto Star*, Getty Images

Page 52: © Jim McKnight

Page 56: © Gail Harvey

Page 62: © Gail Harvey

Page 67: courtesy of the Fox family

Page 68: © Rohanna Mertins for douggoodman.com

Page 74: © Gail Harvey

Page 78: © Donna Fraser

Page 82: © Gail Harvey

Page 88: courtesy of Nadine Caron

Page 94: © Jana Solnickova

Page 100: © Ed Linkewich

Page 104: © Lisa Adams

Page 108: © Martin Tessler Photography

Page 113: Ken Mayer Studio © 2005 Douglas Coupland

Page 114: © Mike Latschislaw

Page 119: Ken Mayer Studio © 2005 Douglas Coupland

Page 120: © Rick Hansen Foundation

Page 125: courtesy of the Fox family

Page 126: © The Terry Fox Laboratory

Page 131: Ken Mayer Studio © 2005 Douglas Coupland

Page 132: © David Cooper / *Toronto Star*, Getty Images

Page 138: © Perdita Felicien

Page 142: courtesy of the Jarvis family

Page 147: courtesy of the Fox family

Page 148: © Jim McKnight

Page 152: © Mark Grimstead

Page 157: courtesy of the Fox family

Page 158: © CTV News

Page 163: © Terry Fox Foundation/courtesy of the Fox family

Page 164: © Mary Hardisty

Page 169: Ken Mayer Studio © 2005 Douglas Coupland

Page 170: © Terry Fox Foundation/courtesy of the Fox family

Page 175: courtesy of the Fox family

Page 176: © Wendy Kennelly

Page 180: © Keith Beaty / *Toronto Star*, Getty Images

Page 185: courtesy of the Fox family

Page 186: © Akshay Grover

Page 191: © Terry Fox Foundation/courtesy of the Fox family

Page 192: courtesy of the Fox family
Page 195: courtesy of the Fox family
Page 196: Ian Muttoo, Flickr / Creative Commons
Page 202: © Tyler Park
Page 207: Ken Mayer Studio © 2005 Douglas Coupland
Page 208: © Gail Harvey
Page 212: © Peter Martin
Page 216: © Debbie Laurie
Page 221: © Terry Fox Foundation/courtesy of the Fox family
Page 222: © Catriona Le May Doan
Page 227: courtesy of the Fox family
Page 228: © *Toronto Star* Archives, Getty Images
Page 233: Ken Mayer Studio © 2005 Douglas Coupland
Page 234: courtesy of the Fox family
Page 237: Material republished with the express
   permission of: *Vancouver Sun*, a division
   of Postmedia Network Inc.
Page 238: courtesy of the Fox family
Page 241: © Terry Fox Foundation/courtesy of the Fox family
Page 244: courtesy of the Fox family
Page 248: © Terry Fox Foundation/courtesy of the Fox family
Page 252: Ken Mayer Studio © 2005 Douglas Coupland

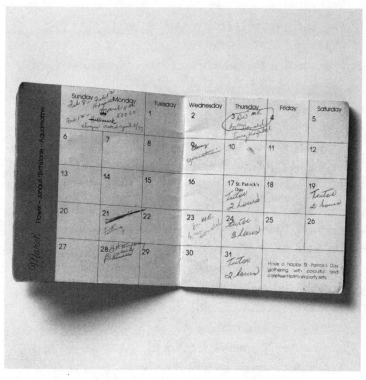

Betty Fox's calendar from March 1977. Betty notes Terry's hospital appointment on March 3rd, when he received his cancer diagnosis, and six days later, the operation to amputate Terry's right leg.

Contributors' Credits

THE FOX FAMILY is deeply committed to keeping Terry's legacy alive. Before he passed away, Terry knew that there would be an annual run in his name and helped to establish the values and vision that the Terry Fox Foundation adheres to and proudly shares today. Betty Fox, with Rolly Fox close by her side, stepped up to speak for Terry when he no longer could, accepting a role in the development of the Terry Fox Run which would later evolve into the Terry Fox Foundation. The Foundation is dedicated to raising funds for cancer research through the efforts of thousands of volunteers across the country and around the world who organize walks, runs, and other fundraising events annually in communities, schools, and corporate offices. The direct descendants of Betty and Rolly Fox fulfill a governance role with the Terry Fox Foundation as members with defined responsibilities and roles. They are also charged with being the lead on initiatives that wish to honour Terry's legacy or communicate his powerful and moving story, such as *Forever Terry*. Darrell Fox, editor of this collection on behalf of the Fox family, is Terry's younger brother.

VIKING
an imprint of Penguin Canada
www.penguinrandomhouse.ca